A Girl in Blue

Lois Willoughby-Easter

BLUE LAMP
BOOKS

First Edition
Copyright © Lois Willoughby-Easter, 2019

The right of Lois Willoughby-Easter to be identified as the author of this work has been asserted in accordance with the Copyright, Designs & Patents Act 1988.

All rights reserved. No part of this book may be reprinted or reproduced or utilised in any form or by any electronic, mechanical or other means, now known or hereafter invented, including photocopying and recording, or in any information storage or retrieval system, without the prior permission in writing of the publishers.

ISBN: 978-1-911273-45-5 (softcover)
ISBN: 978-1-911273-46-2 (ebook)

Published by Blue Lamp Books

An Imprint of
Mango Books
18 Soho Square
London W1D 3QL
www.MangoBooks.co.uk

A Girl in Blue

About the Author

Lois Willoughby-Easter was born in Cheltenham in 1948, but when her parents separated she and her mother relocated to south London. There she attended several schools, but due to her disrupted upbringing her academic achievements were limited. However, after gaining a Bachelor of Education degree with Art at East Anglia Polytechnic in 1990, for 25 years she worked in London as a primary school teacher, determined to try to unlock each child's true potential.

On retirement Lois decided to record the experiences of her early life and the events which, in 1967, led to her becoming a Metropolitan Woman Police Constable at the age of nineteen. Her career was varied, and although Women Police had the same powers of arrest as their male colleagues, Lois often undertook the specialist work which women officers did prior to their integration with their male counterparts in 1973.

Lois lives with her husband, a retired long-serving police officer, in a restored farmhouse in Norfolk. They are both interested in Police history, having carried out much research through the Metropolitan Police historical collection. Lois is also a member of the Metropolitan Women Police Association.

She has had several poems published and is a confident artist, inspired mainly by the wonderful landscapes Norfolk has to offer.

This book is dedicated to the many Police officers
who spend their lives trying to make the streets
in which we live peaceful places. For the most part,
they are honest, over-worked and underpaid,
but they face their duties with a positive attitude
and good humour.

These are the street officers, the detectives and
the undercover heroes who daily put their lives at risk
in order to protect us.

*

My thanks and appreciation also go out to
my husband James and my daughters,
and Daphne and Mandi, who inspired me to write my story
and to all those who enjoy it.

Contents

Introduction	1
Thirties and Forties	3
Early Years	5
South East London Culture Shock	19
Middle Class Suburbia	29
Career Path	39
She's Leaving Home	47
Peto House	49
Peel House	55
Posted to the Sticks	79
The Summer of Love	107
Comrades	111
Policing Romford	127
Hendon Driving School	151
West End Central: Vice Squad	157
Hornchurch Manor	167
Posted to Dagenham	177
Policing P Division	183
'Times They are a Changing'	197
End of an Era	199
Index	203

Introduction

The role of female officers serving with the Metropolitan Police changed forever in 1973 with the so-called integration with their male counterparts; the WPC became a PC, equal in every way except gender. The move was not universally welcomed, however, and not just by male officers.

This book tells the story of my almost six years as a Girl in Blue - a young female police officer serving with the Met in the years immediately before integration. It is a story probably typical of many WPCs who served in the late Sixties and early Seventies, facing what would be seen today as sexism and bullying, and eventually earning the respect of their male peers, although sometimes begrudgingly.

But my years spent with the Met were happy ones and within that time I made lasting friendships. I also learnt important life skills, which have remained with me to this day.

I wouldn't have changed anything for the world, and I hope that in some way I made a difference.

Lois Willoughby-Easter
Norfolk, October 2018

Thirties and Forties

Gert collapsed on the living room sofa. Tears fell from her bespectacled eyes; eyes fixed on the hideous flames where in the grate the aborted foetus turned to glowing embers, then cold grey cinders and finally charcoaled remains. When the compacted towels between her legs had reached saturation point, she lost consciousness.

Fourteen years prior to the termination of this miniature human being, Gert, then aged 21, had married Alf, the son of local Italian immigrants. Their union in 1931 provided her with an escape from her working class background and Alf's job as a men's hairdresser ensured the financial security for which she craved.

After the wedding, in quick succession Gert bore two children; first a daughter, Brenda, followed by a son named Ralph, a deliberate extension of his father's moniker. However, as good a man as Alf was, in time Gert became bored with her suburban lifestyle in Kent where they had moved to from Bermondsey. She was a good-looking and amusing woman, and from time-to-time she would desert the family's three-bedroom terraced home, allegedly to visit her mother and brother in south London. But it was not to the south she would travel, instead heading to the bright lights of west London in search of excitement or perchance an encounter with some like-minded fellow.

Then, during the Victory over Europe Day celebrations on 8th May 1945, Gert was in the Mall when a passing embrace from a man recently demobbed from the Air

A Girl in Blue

Force transformed her life forever.

The opportunity to exchange dour domesticity for a new post-war life in the west country, from where Bill originated, was too hard to resist so Gert deserted Alf and their children to set up home in Cheltenham, Gloucestershire in pursuit of Bill's promised utopia.

Two years later, had Gert managed to repeat the illegal termination of an unwanted pregnancy I may have come to a premature end, but thankfully I survived to relate my story.

*

> I remember, I remember
> The house where I was born,
> The little window where the sun
> Came peeping in at morn;
>
> - Thomas Hood

On Candlemas Day, February 2nd 1948, I contributed to the famed post-war birth rate and was safely delivered, pre the National Health Service, by a private doctor on my parents' double bed. I was told later that I weighed no more than a 2lb bag of sugar, Tate & Lyle granulated I presume, so seemingly my delivery went without much ado although my survival may have been seriously undermined as the gales, thunderstorms and low temperatures on that day were widely reported throughout the British Isles.

Fortunately, I was lovingly tucked up in a blue woollen honeycomb blanket, I think they might have been expecting a son, in an open drawer of my father's bureau for at least the first few weeks of my life, during which justifiably, Alf filed for divorce.

Forties and Fifties

Early Years

The house where I was born was purchased by Bill at the end of the Second World War. It was a substantial Regency-style property called the Royston situated at the Montpellier end of Cheltenham, a spa town and borough located on the edge of the Cotswolds.[1]

At birth, I was given a not-so-well known name from the New Testament where Paul mentions Lois as the pious grandmother in his second epistle to Timothy. Even though my mother had no particular religious leanings, as a young woman she worked as a domestic servant for a devout Jewish family in London so it may be that she had remembered the name 'Lois' for possible future use. Jane was added as my middle name in honour of Emily Jane, my paternal grandmother, a woman I

---

1 In the late 1800s William Nash Skillicorne, the first mayor of the town, resided in the house. He was the great grandson of Captain Henry Skillicorne (1678-1763), generally considered to be the founding father of modern Cheltenham. He developed the Spa in what is known as Royal Well and just off the promenade a private garden bears his name. In 1999, nearly 150 years later, I attended a Blue Plaque ceremony when one was installed on 'Royston', 9 Queen's Parade, as a permanent marker to commemorate William Skillicorne's former residence. According to the 1911 census, William Maud Skillicorne was still in the house aged 50 with his 87-year-old mother Mary Ann and his sisters Edith and Elizabeth. They had a cook, two house parlourmaids and a live-in nurse for Mary Ann; visions of a life gone by.

never met as she had died some years before I arrived in the world.

At first some may have questioned my lineage, but there could be no doubt I was my father's child. I had the same slim physique and eyes the same sea blue as his. We had similar high foreheads and a cow's lick wave at the front of our poker-straight hair.

Despite the religious connection with my name, no-one ever arranged for me to be Christened, perhaps never able to find the time. But despite the questionable choices mother made in her life she resolutely taught me right from wrong, and encouraged me to treat others with respect.

By the time I was three or four years old I had taken to the grandeur of my surroundings with aplomb. I was aware of the high ceilings in the rooms of the Royston, each elaborately fashioned with ornate plaster coving, sculpted like icing on a wedding cake. And, rising a foot or so from the floor, painted wainscots skirted richly-papered walls.

I was blissfully unaware, however, of how much my mother toiled to support my father in his business. Apparently, after only having met her a couple of times, he had discovered that in her late teens she had studied Domestic Science at Goldsmith's College and realised what a great asset she would be to him as he developed the Royston into a hotel.

Although I had no understanding of my illegitimacy I did sometimes consider myself to be an inconvenience to my parents, so I learned the places in the hotel where I could lurk unnoticed. One of my favourite pursuits, oblivious of the danger involved, was to slide down the banister rail of the grand sweeping staircase from the first floor to the entrance hall, where my journey was halted on a curl of polished oak.

When my half-brother Ralph came to visit during his school holidays we would play hide-and-seek upstairs in the house or downstairs in the basement, evading capture anywhere we could. One basement staircase led to the former servants' quarters, where high up on the wall was a row of twenty bells with a room number above each one. This contraption would have been activated by anyone who required the assistance of downstairs staff, quite in the style of television's *Upstairs Downstairs* or *Downton Abbey*.

During our time in the hotel most of the bedrooms were let out to paying guests, so my mother was expected to manage all the household chores without the help of modern-day appliances and also prepare meals for those who wanted them. White linen sheets and damask tablecloths would be boiled, dunked in vats of milk-coloured starch, then put through the ringer, dried on wooden clothes-horses and finally smoothed with a heavy flat iron heated on the stove. She laboriously polished brass stair-rods which secured red Axminster treads on the four flights of stairs from the entrance hall to the attic. She once told me she had seen the ghostly apparition of a lady descending the staircase; I wonder now if it had been a visitation from one of the Skillicornes.

Another of the many chores with which my mother had to cope was the cleaning of the chicken shed, which held more than a few domestic hens.

'I hate this job,' mother would grumble, 'the smell of chicken shit stays on me for days.'

'But Mum, I like collecting the warm eggs from the

nest boxes.'

My humble response seemed to afford her sufficient justification for carrying out this painstaking task where the dropping boards, the sullied straw, perches and boxes had to be scrubbed clean.

Then when one or more of our large flock of free range chickens was required for the kitchen, my father would break the neck of the chosen victim and plunge it into boiling water.

'Your turn now, to pluck out the feathers.' he would call.

Some children might have shied away from such a command, but I relished any opportunity to learn anything interesting and new.

'Grab a feather like this,' he would demonstrate, 'and pull it out. You'll get the hang of it after you've plucked a few. The faster you work, the easier the feathers will come out, because the skin will still be loose. Of course, the more pinfeathers there are the harder this will be.'

So the still-warm dead chicken would land on my lap for plucking to commence.

'Once all the feathers and pinfeathers are out, there will still be some light hairy ones on the chicken. Afterwards I will have to singe them off over a gas flame,' he explained.

'What will you do with all the feathers?'

'I'll get your mother to clean them and use them to stuff pillows.' As if she hadn't enough tasks to complete.

Like most children my concentration span tended to be short, but I was determined to pluck at least one chicken before wandering off to entertain myself elsewhere in the garden. That often meant climbing the brick wall of the pigsty to watch our sow wallowing in the mud with her piglets. Or I would leap over the garden's manicured box hedges, pretending to be a jockey on horseback at the Cheltenham Races. I had been taken to the races on a few occasions and remember standing close to my parents beside the race track as the horses' hooves thundered by; a seemingly terrifying experience for a small child, but I wondered at the blurred, colourful silks as they sped past.

Other times I would drive my blue pedal car around the extensive garden pretending to be a policeman, imagining I was chasing robbers or stopping to let pedestrians cross in front of me. On hot summer days I might sit on the lawn in the shade of an ancient mulberry tree and sample its luscious purple blue fruit, or I would watch our hired gardener as he dug the earth and gathered produce for our dining table.

'What you doing, Ben?'

'Digging up 'tatoes for yer supper, my love.'

In the summertime, Ben would let me pick the well-tended soft fruit. However, one time when eating the delicious berries the rash I developed so alarmed mother that she suspected scarlet fever. But after obtaining medical advice the itchy hives were diagnosed as an overindulgence of strawberries.

In spite of the hard work my mother had encountered there were opportunities for relaxation.

At weekends, whatever the weather, my father would drive mother and I, and Ralph and Brenda when they visited, to explore the picturesque Cotswolds.

His black Standard Flying 8 motor-car was his pride and joy. I know it was a Standard model as I vividly recall the metal Union Jack emblem that such cars had on their bonnet. It was a sturdy affair with roomy leather seats and a running board step to assist us five passengers to board the vehicle. As a special treat my father would sit me on his lap whist driving – years before health and safety concerns - to allow me to take the steering wheel and salute a passing AA man in his mustard yellow uniform if one happened to pass by on his motorbike.

Because a lot of my time was spent alone, I had taught myself to read well before school age by frequently immersing myself in the poems in one of the few books I owned entitled Shakespeare to Hardy, a well-worn publication I had found inside a box of my father's auction house purchases. Later on I became an avid reader of Enid Blyton's Secret Seven and Famous Five stories, so full of mystery and intrigue. As a five year old, audaciously I once wrote to Miss Blyton questioning something she had written in one of her stories. She kindly replied explaining details of the plot which satisfied and cheered me up immensely.

As well as looking after the domestic side of the Royston, my mother had to manage a former public house called Crispin Villa that was purchased by my father in New Street, at the lower, less salubrious end of Cheltenham. She and I moved into part of the property while four or five of the other bedrooms in the property were rented to Irish navvies or nurses. Once again the demands of running such an establishment were huge, but I remained unaware of this and continued my childhood fantasies. Davy Crockett was the superhero of the day and the must-have accessory for a young child was a Davy Crockett hat - mock racoon fur with an attached tail. And if I happened to be playing out in the street with one or two like-minded bow and arrow and toy gun wielding cowboys, I had to be the sheriff!

My parents had little idea about my childish pursuits, but they did notice my enthusiasm for learning, so at age four-and-a-half I was enrolled in St. Gregory's primary school close to where we lived. None of my family was Catholic, but because my father's pub skittles companion was the Head Teacher of the school I was readily accepted into a seemingly good Christian education. And being an only child, I was delighted at last to be in the company of other children, although as it turned out my learning curve to acceptable behaviour was steep.

The majority of the teaching staff at St Gregory's were nuns, so I was soon to discover that those who taught me were either kind and good or out-and-out tyrants. My first teacher, the formidable Sister Bernadette, did not fit the saintly picture my mother had painted of those who had taken vows of poverty, chastity and obedience. The nun in question had it in for me from the moment I arrived. But it was during one particular arithmetic lesson, when I was given a large blue card that displayed the required number of dots and the accompanying number digit, when things began to get serious. It did not occur to me that I should not wave the card like a fan in the face of one of my fellow infants. Without further ado, Sister Bernadette's Irish brogue resounded around the classroom.

'Come out here at once you little divil!' she boomed as she produced a whipping cane from beside her chair.

I had never seen a cane before but instinctively I knew what was going to happen to me was not going to be pleasant. However, I was determined not to show the horrid teacher any signs of fear and stoically held out my tiny palm to meet the cane as it thwacked down.

Naturally this was excruciating but I forced back the tears, not wanting to let the rest of the class see my pain. Afterwards Sister Bernadette glared at me and then at the rest of the class of trembling five-year-olds and snarled, 'You are all going to behave yourselves now, aren't you?'

Later the same day, as I walked down the corridor on my way to my classroom, Sister Agnes held her arms across her ample chest, lifted up her head, peered over her glasses and remarked, 'Hello, young lady. What have you been up to?'

Agnes was one of the kindest and serene members of the sisterly order, but it was clear to me she knew what had happened. I felt very humiliated and believed God had told everyone, because otherwise how could she know? Was she going to tell my father or the Head Teacher, Mr. Rawlins? My only hope was that he and my father were out somewhere playing skittles.

Throughout my time in Sister Bernadette's class her attitude toward me never changed, even though I did my best not to mishandle any of the class equipment. But one day I arrived at school wearing bright blue shoes.

'Holy Mary, Mother of God, what are you wearing on your feet?'

'My new shoes,' I answered with pride.

'You are only allowed black shoes, your mother should know that is the rule.'

'My mother can only afford to buy shoes that I can wear for school, and for best.'

'Child you are being very insolent.'

I dared not say anything more, as another unjust punishment needed to be avoided at all costs. I really loved my new blue shoes, for which my feet had been measured with precision in a machine in the children's shoe shop in the centre of town.[2]

Early Years

I still remember how the friendly assistant placed my newly blue shod feet into a slot at the bottom of this box. Peering through a hole at the top, I could see the skeleton of my feet inside the outline of the new shoes. The attendant and my mother peered through other holes, encouraging me to wiggle my toes, making sure there was ample space.[2]

So as far as Sister Bernadette was concerned, uniform shoes I had to have. So mother returned me to the shop for a pair of Startrite, regulation black.

One Christmas Sister Bernadette decided to cast her pupils in a Nativity play. Julie Garland was chosen to be Mary and it was she who was to wear the traditional white robe and blue headdress, and Lionel Wood was chosen as Joseph. To my utter disappointment I was to be a sheep. If I couldn't have been Mary I desperately wanted to be an angel, but there was no way Sister Bernadette would have considered that. In rehearsals we children learnt *Hark the Herald Angels*, singing it over and over until we got every word as clear as a bell.

Sister Bernadette also had an absolute abhorrence for anybody who didn't know how to pronounce the word 'angels' properly:

---

2   Years later, I learnt that the Pedoscope was marketed as a sure-fire method of ensuring well-fitting shoes and healthy feet. The mystery wooden box held an X-ray tube in a lead-shielded base beneath the platform the customer stood on. At the push of a button, a beam travelled up through the feet, and an image of the bones within the outline of the new shoes was directed onto a fluorescent screen. Even the shoe's stitching could be seen. Shoe shops and their customers loved the Pedoscope, which was in use for four decades from the 1920s onwards. 10,000 machines were installed in America, about 3,000 in Britain and 1,500 in Switzerland, the home of Bally, once the world's largest shoe manufacturer. For children like me, bored with the dreary chore of shoe-shopping, the X-ray machine was attractive and as exciting as being handed a free balloon. By the Fifties concern was growing about the potential hazards of Pedoscopes so the machine was eventually phased out.

'Angels is NOT pronounced an-gels [as in the gel you put in your hair]; it is pronounced an-juls!'

If anybody did not adhere to such instruction, her jaw would clamp shut and her eyes would slit like snakes. She would make examples of any of us, especially rotund Johnny Green.

One day whilst the class was standing in line in the main hall waiting for assembly to begin, Johnny whispered how he hated school. Nothing got passed Bernadette.

'Johnny, come out here at once. YOU can say the prayer today, and it had better be worthy.'

I saw Johnny tremble, but being the good Catholic boy he was he managed to utter something the Sister found acceptable.

Maybe if I had been able to get in touch with the Pope to tell him how unbearable Sister Bernadette was, and how she tended to flirt outrageously with Father What's-his-name, that would have shown her! Father What's-his-name used to visit our classroom often, and we watched the serpent turn into a coy young woman, shrugging her shoulders, batting her eyelashes, swaying or perhaps swooning and smiling, her face red with blush. I was confused by such behaviour, and I so wanted to let the Pope know that one of his flock was not behaving like the nun she ought to be. But I didn't know the Pope's phone number.

As luck would have it, I missed the Nativity play all together. Instead, still only five-years-old, I was admitted to Cheltenham General Hospital to have my tonsils removed. I was taken there by my mother and then left alone in an austere ward with only my doll as company, a doll with large hoop earrings and facial features embroidered in colours befitting an African native. I loved her.

The day of my operation I had to leave my companion at the foot of my bed, and I was taken in a thin white gown by one of the nurses and made to sit in a glass kiosk where my teeth chattered and my legs shook violently with fear before my pre-med injection was administered and I was taken to surgery. When I surfaced from my ordeal, bloodied and bruised around my mouth, I vowed that I would try never to be so afraid again, whatever the circumstances.

Needless to say I soon recovered and continued to be occupied with school, the house and what the vast gardens had to offer, but sometimes I would step outside onto the pavement to wonder what lay beyond the wide, tree-lined, traffic-free avenue. My imagination would run riot. I would travel to the farthest corners of the world. I wanted to grow up and do something good.

I was born in the reign of George VI, but after his untimely death in 1952 a particular highlight during my infant years was the Coronation of his daughter Elizabeth. Celebrations took place throughout the land, and I especially recall the St Gregory's school assembly where all the children and staff had to wear something in national colours. My mother dressed my hair in pigtails secured with ribbon bows of red, white and blue and she also knitted me a pair of similarly coloured woollen socks, but although I enjoyed the patriotism of the occasion, the socks were incredibly itchy.

Some solace was attained that June day, when a representative of Cheltenham Borough Council presented every child with a commemorative spoon, the handle of which displayed an impression of Her Majesty.

Television really came into its own for the Coronation

of Elizabeth II. Permission had been granted for television cameras to film in Westminster Abbey and sales of televisions rocketed. But as my family did not own a television, our neighbour invited my mother and I into her front room to watch the event on her set, a nine-inch Bakelite 'Bush' model, in front of which several residents from adjoining houses huddled round in awe to see the young Queen of England. In fact it wasn't until I was ten years of age that my mother did manage to purchase our own television with simply just two channels, BBC and ITV.

Then there were the Brownies. At first I wasn't sure what they did, but I had seen other small girls sporting the brown uniform and I was eager to be part of it all. So I joined the local pack and in due course was enrolled:

'I promise that I will do my best, to do my duty to God and the Queen, to help other people every day especially those at home.'

Each week I readily accepted the challenges set by the Brown Owl and quickly began to accrue Brownie badges to sew onto the sleeve of my uniform. The most useful one I recall was successfully setting a table, something which remained with me throughout my life. Woe betides anyone who places an item of cutlery on the table in the wrong place!

My time at St Gregory's School had a welcome intermission, for my father decided to take my mother and I on a trip through Europe. Being the successful businessman he was, he was able to afford a hot-off-the-production-line Bedford Dormobile van to add to his fleet of vehicles. He left his business ventures in the hands of Mr Middleton, his solicitor, and early in 1955 we set off from icy England to camp throughout France and southern Spain, where on the rock of Gibraltar I celebrated my 7th birthday. Thereafter we visited Italy and Germany, the mountains of Switzerland, Belgium and Luxembourg. It greatly satisfied my father's lust for travel and the whole trip was a unique experience for each of us. After three months we returned home, but our future deemed less favourable.

Although at the time I never knew why my parents quarrelled, I was aware that their relationship was becoming more and more turbulent, and one day I looked on in horror when, screaming like a banshee, mother was chasing my father around the hotel garden brandishing a horse whip. So when my grandmother informed my mother that rooms had become available for us in her back-to-back terraced house in Bermondsey, south east London the offer was readily accepted. So it was with a new purpose that mother and I, aged eight, packed what possessions we could fit into a brown leather suitcase and, without a backward glance, caught a Black and White Company coach destined for London.

My mother was born in the house in 1910 and I had visited several times so we both thought the move would not be too onerous. Furthermore, I was pleased to learn that we would be living in the converted upstairs flat rather than actually with my grandmother for whenever we had visited her she would always be sitting solemnly in the scullery in front of the dying embers of an open coal fire, the skirt of her faded floral pinafore straining across her thighs as she parted her plump brown stocking-covered legs to maximise her share of what little heat there was in the flames that struggled up the soot-lined chimney. For years she had struggled to raise her family, often devoid of the support of her husband. Little is known about how she and Frederick Robert Hunt, who had been born in

A Girl in Blue

Peckham in 1884, got together, but seemingly they met at a social gathering or through relatives. He worked on the railways as a lighterman on the river. Then in 1917, at the age of 33, he did his duty for King and Country serving as a Lance Corporal in the Royal Engineers. However, due to somehow sustaining a ruptured hernia and a head injury whilst in France, he was invalided out and sent home to recover in the London General Hospital in Denmark Hill, which contained 231 beds for officers and 1,038 for enlisted men. Thereafter, the nearby local pub The Bramcote Arms afforded some medicinal relief, but his family were all the poorer for it.

In the early twentieth century all working-class districts of London were crowded with such establishments, as they provided a friendly home-from-home. Plenty of gas-light and roaring fires made them often much more comfortable than people's miserable hovels, and many men could barely be prised away from the pub. But when Frederick did get home he would enlist the comfort of his wife, hence the children that arrived in quick succession my mother being the eldest of the seven.

On one of my earlier visits to the house, a few days before Easter - I would have been just over two - I recall being carried by my mother to see my grandfather lying on a single bed in a downstairs room. The air was heavy with the smell of camphor, and dusty velvet curtains were drawn to keep out the morning light. He died that Good Friday.

1956

South East London Culture Shock

In Bermondsey my mother settled quickly into familiar surroundings.

I was enrolled in a school at the end of the street, Ilderton Road Juniors, the same one my mother had attended as a child. But compared with the pupils at my Gloucestershire County School, these were definitely different. I was not readily accepted by them and one day, when I had only been at the school a few weeks, I was followed home by twin girls who were pupils in my class.

'What yer doin rand ere? Ya posh caw.'

Betty and Beatie took turns in repeating their taunts, but as I reached the front door of my home I suddenly flew into a rage, turned and to their absolute surprise I lashed out at the girls, striking each of them on their jaw with my fist. My retaliation caused me to seek the protection of my own front door and since it was always left ajar for me to enter after school, I ran inside and they slumped off down the street. The twins never bothered me again, but in order for me to be accepted into the community in which I was to stay for an unspecified amount of time I decided that my Gloucestershire accent had to go. Furthermore, in order to eradicate any association with my father, my mother had my name changed by deed poll from Clark to that of her married name of Willoughby.

Along with my new identity, everything in my young life was now an assortment of good and not-so-good.

My grandmother's house was small compared with the homes we had left behind, and furthermore I did not take to having to sleep in the same double bed as my mother. The upstairs front bedroom had a double and a single bed and two large dark oak wardrobes along one wall. To access the toilet, one had go downstairs and out of the scullery door into the back yard. The draughty shed had a scrubbed wooden bench seat and central hole, and from a sitting position I observed some kind of fungus, a bit like mushrooms, growing out of various places in the whitewashed brickwork. Prepared squares of torn newspaper hung from a rusty hook on the back of the door, in vast contrast to the Royston's crisp sheets of Izal, and I loathed going to the outside privy at any time but especially in the dead of night. At least there was the bedroom chamber pot alternative.

As well as having no inside toilet my grandmother's house had no bathroom either, unlike the well-appointed ones of the Royston Hotel, so I would be bathed in an oval galvanised tin bath brought in from its hanging space outside on the garden fence. The water would be heated in a boiler in grandmother's scullery before I was placed in the bath in front of the living room open coal fire. This was not a pleasant experience, for one side of my body would get red and blotchy from the heat of the fire while the other side of me got cold. Occasionally mother could afford us the luxury of going to the public footbaths together to purge ourselves, something I looked forward to immensely.

South East London Culture Shock

At the footbaths mother would ask for two entry tickets:

'Sixpence each,' demanded the portly male attendant. 'Towels on the left. Ladies to the right.'

The towels were sumptuous, snowy-white Egyptian cotton, and after collecting them we were each ushered into our designated narrow cubicle. The cavernous white-enamelled bath had a big shiny water spout at one end - the water was adjusted from the outside by the female attendant in the corridor. She would put in the appropriate mix of hot and cold, but if it was not of a suitable temperature one would have to shout, 'More hot in number 4!' or 'More cold in number 6!'

There were no facilities for drying one's hair in the baths, so during the winter mother and I would stop off in the interior of our local chippy to watch fresh fish and chips being cooked in bubbling hot fat whilst drying ourselves off some more in the warm air. Then the delicious fayre was drenched in salt and vinegar and wrapped in newspaper to form a hot parcel, which we broke open and ate on the way home. If finances didn't extend to this traditional partnership then chips alone were just as welcome. In the summer however, a special treat was to buy a lemon ice for one penny from Joe's, the Italian ice cream parlour on the corner of Ilderton Road and Zampa Road. It was run by genuine Italian immigrants Joe and his wife Lou and their two sons Vinnie and Tony.

Such were the adjustments I had to accept in London, but often I would look out into the street from the bay window of 123 Verney Road's parlour, thinking about the friends and the life I had left behind. The parlour was a gloomy room lit only at night by an electric light that struggled to shine through its mottled glass shade where, only a few years earlier, a gas mantle had hung. In an alcove beside the open coal fireplace stood an old upright piano that triggered reminders of my days with Miss Sweet, my music teacher who used to visit our house in Cheltenham every Friday after school to teach me piano. Her rose-scented face powder endeared her to me as much as her name.

'Your daughter is a prodigy,' Miss Sweet would proclaim, 'such a gifted child.'

Although I enjoyed the process of learning, I think her opinion of me was somewhat exaggerated and only served to nurture her own self-worth.

So in the parlour I would sit down on the worn velvet seat of the accompanying stool and lift the piano lid to release a musty aroma, like a genie escaping from its bottle. My right hand practised a major scale on the discoloured ivory keys. C-D-E-F; the G was silent; A was very out of tune, while B sometimes worked and sometimes didn't, although none of this mattered as piano lessons in Bermondsey were no longer affordable.

*

In response to the demands made by my father, my mother would occasionally take me to the local telephone to phone him. The phone box stood near the Grand Surrey Canal Bridge, from where, my mother related how in 1936 she had surveyed the crimson sky over the Crystal Palace as it was razed to the ground.

En-route to the phone box she and I would walk past identical Victorian terraced houses typical of working-class south east London and we would play a game of trying not to step on any of the cracks between the

South East London Culture Shock

pavement slabs.

'If you step on one, you won't really run off with a stranger will, you Mum?'

She assured me she wouldn't.

My mother's response was temporarily comforting, for having lost one parent I needed all the reassurance she could proffer.

We were not close in the tactile sense but she was always protective of me, and it must have pained her greatly to walk away from the good life she had been promised in Cheltenham. Latterly it was disappointing to realise that if things had worked out differently, after St Gregory's Primary School my education would most likely have continued at Cheltenham Ladies' College, my father could have afforded to send me there, but unfortunately that chapter of my life was not meant to be.

As we walked together along the road mother would tell me about her life when she was one of the Bermondsey kids, and I was quite taken with her recollections for I had little idea of how poor her upbringing actually was.

'There was no money for expensive toys; the adults were too busy dealing with their own hardships to set anything up for us. We expected nothing but enjoyed ourselves.'

'What did you play back then Mum?'

She pondered whilst delving into her memory bank.

'I used to play marbles. Just here in fact,' pointing to the grimey gutters. 'Spheres of glass with swirls of coloured threads trapped inside that rolled and crashed, rattled over drain covers.'

She recalled how schoolboys with faces as dirty as hers would call to her, 'Four-eyes Gerty from number thirty!'

But they soon learned that she, the eldest and most

resilient child in her family from a similarly deprived background, could give as well as they sent, and more. She was no shrinking violet, and from an early age it would seem that she definitely had leanings towards improved rights for the fairer sex. In 1918 she would have been eight years old when the Suffragette movement was in full swing. Ten years later, when the Conservative government passed the Representation of the People Act giving the vote to all women over the age of 21, I am sure Gert would liked to have been first in the queue but had to wait a few years more.

'What other games, Mum?'

'Well if we could get hold of someone's whip and top that was fun or we would play leapfrog or knock down Ginger.'

All these pursuits encapsulated the pastimes of Edwardian children who were expected to entertain themselves. Fortunately there was little or no traffic then, so the street was their playground: the roads, the pavements, and minimal gardens.

Adulthood and marriage had allowed my mother to escape this working-class community, but in due course she was back where she started, and this time with me.

The Bermondsey streets were now my playground too. In the 1950s there were still few cars in the back streets. No one I knew except my father had a car and he was miles away, so it was perfectly safe to play out. The bomb site opposite my grandmother's house was the adventure playground for us local children, but the vacant derelict ground was a terrible reminder to those residents who had lived through the intense attacks on the nearby Surrey Docks only ten years before.

On reaching the telephone box I would run ahead of

mother to pull open the heavy door of the kiosk from where my father could be contacted. Inside we dropped copper pennies into the coin slot one by one before we dialled his number.

'You hold the receiver,' mother said as she handed me the weighty, black Bakelite object, 'I'll press button 'A' when he answers.'

'Hello Daddy, it's me.'

'Hello me.'

'How are you? What have you been up to?' was my usual introduction to our conversation.

'I've been to the pictures.'

Visiting the cinema had been a favourite pastime of ours before I had been relocated to London.

'What have you seen?' I asked eagerly.

'*Seven Brides for Seven Brothers*. A musical. And *Genevieve*, you'd have liked that as I did. Was all about a race in the annual London to Brighton antique car rally.'

Whatever the film, I loved the cinema. Although the British Board of Film Censors was established in 1912 by the film industry, local authorities imposed widely varying censorship standards on films so I was able to see most popular films of the day, even those directed by Hitchcock, but I particularly relished those with the most suspense whilst happily sitting on a plush red velvet cinema seat, tucking blindly into a toffee-filled brown paper bag.

'Where were they on?' I asked.

'At The Daffodil, the Art Deco one at the one at the top end of Montpellier,' he paused a moment 'and The Regal, you remember, on the Promenade opposite the Neptune Fountain, where you used to go to see Saturday morning pictures.'

'Oh, I remember.'

On Saturday mornings I had been allowed to go to the ABC in Cheltenham, a major Saturday cinema club for children, where I became a member of the ABC Minors. At the beginning of each Saturday morning session, the ABC Minors' Song would be played to the tune of *Blaze Away* by Abe Holzmann while a bouncing red ball danced above the projected lyrics on the screen to help the kids join in.

'I miss us sharing sweets, especially the liquorice sticks. Mummy didn't like your mouth getting all black. Have you lost any more teeth recently?'

'A couple, but Mummy says the fairies round here haven't got a lot of spare cash.'

I looked up at my mother who was straining to listen to the conversation.

'That's enough about pictures,' she said, snatching the receiver from my hand.

My mother had only ever seen *Gone with the Wind* and thought it far too long, and chose never to visit a cinema again.

Although the calls to my father were infrequent, he did manage to lure mother and I to Cheltenham once again where he subsequently proposed and presented her with a substantial diamond engagement ring.

At the same time as this sentimental revelation he was in the process of building a three-bedroom high-specification dwelling for the three of us above the stables in the grounds of the Royston Hotel. We moved in when it was finished and savoured the ultra-modern open plan interior design, and moreover I had a bedroom of my own.

Then, after a couple of months, without any prior

warning my father casually announced that the new dwelling was not actually for mother and I, and told us to leave. We were to be replaced by a middle-aged nurse he had met during a short spell he had spent in hospital and with whom he had subsequently been having an affair.

As a result of this major shock, in 1956 mother took my father to Tower Bridge Court for Breach of Promise, when such laws existed. There she won damages, and moreover kept the ring!

'Heaven has no rage like love to hatred turned, nor hell a fury like a woman scorned!'[3]

---

3   William Congreve, *The Mourning Bride*, 1697. Act III Scene 8.

Fifties and Sixties
Middle Class Suburbia

After we had returned once more to Bermondsey, my half sister Brenda decided to leave her brother and father in Bexley and joined us. She had acquired a job as a cashier at Lloyds Bank in Peckham, south east London, and in a short while mother began seeing Douglas Brignall, the then-Manager of the same branch. During World War II he had served as a Major in the Royal Ordnance Corps in India and mother was keen to get to know him better. He was separated from his French wife because while he was away serving in India she entertained other men, and once back on Civvie Street he left her and was living a solitary existence in a flat in Streatham. Mother orchestrated a meeting with Douglas and before long he was visiting us in Bermondsey and, being free agents, it was not long before he suggested that the three of us should move in together.

First we took up residence in a spacious three-bedroom rented flat in Sydenham, then after about a year he purchased a detached three-bedroom house for the grand sum of £6,000 in a third of an acre in a nearby smart suburban street.

Our situation was now very far removed from SE16, but I wonder if, after all the disappointments my mother and I had experienced in Cheltenham, she had any reservations about this episode of her life, even though she was going to make the most of her superior lifestyle having morphed into a middle-class common-law wife who continued to be a homemaker, but this time on her own terms. Furthermore, Douglas had been promoted to a larger branch of Lloyds Bank in Wandsworth.

Meanwhile he tried not to get too involved with my upbringing, but being a well-educated man he was somewhat disappointed with my academic achievements but probably realised it was ostensibly caused by my fragmented upbringing. After St Gregory's there was St Francis' Primary in Peckham, then Ilderton Road Primary. Next Collingwood, an all-girl secondary modern in New Cross, south east London, and finally I was enrolled at the local school, a state-of-the-art building designed in the 1950s by the famed architect Sir Basil Spence.

So at age twelve I joined the second year to take up my continued secondary education. I had the pre-conceived notion that the young women pupils of Sydenham comprehensive school would be more refined than those of working-class New Cross, and at first I was not to be disappointed. Madame Leblanc, the form tutor of the top stream in the school was charming, and introduced me to her class of well-behaved pupils. However, when they heard my name I noticed an air of unease amongst them, especially from one girl in particular. So I was relieved to know it was not her I had to sit next to, but a different twelve-year-old with a welcoming smile. We remained in class until break-time, when in the playground my new acquaintance introduced herself as Marilyn, but suddenly a small group of girls from our class surrounded us. Then one of them spoke directly at me. 'We already have a Lois in this class – me.' She continued sternly: 'So there is no room for another one.' This was definitely not the reception I was expecting. But because your last name is Willoughby we have decided that you will from this day on be known as Willow. OK?'

I thought it best to readily accept their demand, for I did not know what else they might have had in store. But thankfully, I had been handed an olive branch and Marilyn and the five young women invited me to be in their gang. Our friendship continued throughout our schooldays and beyond into adulthood.

As a thirteen year old I joined the Girl Guides where I was again destined to don a uniform: navy-blue serge skirt and lighter blue cotton shirt on which to attach various acquired badges, and a navy-blue beret completed the look. During this time I had my first foray into camping outdoors. The Guide troop took off in a box-van containing a group of excited giggly teenagers from Sydenham. We were surrounded by tents and camping equipment as we travelled to a camp site in Cudham in Kent. We set up camp in a large field where tent erection, cooking and cleaning rotas were established, but the activity I enjoyed and found most interesting was tracking, one of the traditional scouting pursuits where signs or symbols made from natural material on a trail have to be deciphered.

Camp week proved to be the longest I had ever been away from home, but I had had a taste of freedom and looked forward to any further trips I might be allowed to go on.

I can't say I particularly enjoyed my school years. They came and went, but were greatly enhanced by being able to go on yearly school journeys paid for by Douglas to

Czechoslovakia, Greece, USA and Canada.

But it was in the Art Department where I was at my happiest, dabbling with paint or clay but, knowing my aptitude for creative studies, mother would remark, 'You don't have to go to work when you leave school, there will be plenty of time for that! Neither Douglas or I want you to even think about going to Art College.'

As much as I had considered the Arts, such a career choice would have been far too left wing for either mother or Douglas to accept. Also, my mother's protective attitude and her reluctance to recognise the opportunities that the 1960s offered women nurtured my lack of enthusiasm for education, so although the Sydenham Girls School motto was 'Aim High', those were dizzy heights I failed to reach.

One could sense my teachers' despair by the various ways they would write 'Must try harder' in my reports. However, the teachers who did have some faith in my abilities encouraged me to study Pitman's shorthand and typing in the Commercial Studies lessons to at least prepare me for an office job. Most girls in my year who had already left school were doing just that.

My interest in the opposite sex came at around fourteen, through visits to the local youth club or by mixing socially with the boys from the nearby secondary modern school in Forest Hill. Dates of sorts took me to watch a film at the local cinema, where there nothing more than a kiss or cuddle happened in the back row. But if I arrived home a minute after my ten o'clock curfew I would find my mother at the gate ready to halt any further embraces my escort might have had in mind. As a rebellious teenager I faced many a showdown with my mother. I threatened to leave home - leaping out of the frying pan into the fire comes to mind - but in the main I had to accept her goodly intentions.

By the summer of 1966 I decided I had to do something about my future, for I was eighteen years old and the only student in the Second Year Sixth. Before I actually left school my mother, despite her general reluctance about me working, did allow me take a position that I had seen advertised in the *South London Press* asking for a Saturday night canteen assistant during Bingo sessions above Burton's the tailors in Lewisham. The catering manager at the time was Ivy, a portly middle-aged woman who took me on and professed to have been in catering 'All me life.' I later discovered that she cleaned the public toilets in the centre of Lewisham during the rest of the week.

'The job you've been taken on for lovey is to serve refreshments to the customers in the interval.'

That was what I was expecting to do.

'You know how to make tea?' Ivy asked.

'Yes.'

'Well coffee is a bit trickier.'

Ivy showed me the sparkling clean Gaggia coffee machine. It didn't look too complicated, and after a brief demonstration I realised she would expect me to keep it in the condition to which she was accustomed.

'What time do they come out of the Bingo?' I asked.

"Bout 'alf past eight. But before that you make sure you get all the cups out ready and learn the prices.'

After the players had been refreshed and returned to the adjoining hall, I was told by Ivy to wash up, scrub surfaces, shine the coffee maker and put away all the crockery whilst she sneaked off to play Bingo in the second half! After three Saturdays, I decided catering and the miserly half a crown I was paid was definitely not for me.

My next Saturday job was serving behind the counter of a local chemist owned by a pharmacist called Mr Mott. I was paid five shillings a day to serve customers with over-the-counter medications, cosmetics and toiletries. Problems sometimes arose if a male customer came in to make a discreet purchase. On seeing a young female counter assistant they would shuffle nervously from one foot to the other, then whisper 'Can I speak to the Pharmacist?'

I soon learnt what such customers wanted to purchase, but to avoid any unnecessary embarrassment Mr Mott would descend a short flight of wooden steps from his Dickensian dispensary and without further ado hand 'a packet of three' to the self-conscious customer. Only the very daring might ask me for condoms, sometimes solely to see my reaction, but I quickly learnt to remain stoic.

Overall I enjoyed the work and sometimes, Mr Mott would allow me to dispense prescription tablets or mix the odd potion, and due to his calm encouragement I fleetingly considered studying Pharmacy but felt I could not possibly be confined to the four walls of a High Street store.

On Saturday nights my parents would occasionally allow me to go to one of the south London Mod clubs. One particularly popular club was the Glenlyn in Forest Hill, a snooker hall by day and a cellar dance hall by night: an exciting magnet for the young. Music and fashion were closely linked, dress transformed by new ideas emerging from London's pop scene. Guys would wear tailored, tonic mohair suits and Hush Puppy shoes completed their look, whilst the girls, myself included,

Middle Class Suburbia

followed Mary Quant's influential designs.

The Who, The Rolling Stones, The Byrds and many of the groups starting to tour London appeared at the Glenlyn Ballroom on the minimal stage, raised only a couple of feet from the grimy woodblock dance floor, upon which we shuffled in a crowded, stuffy cigarette or cannabis-infused haze. Amphetamine-fueled drugs, known as Purple Hearts, were easy to obtain from known suppliers within the club, but that was an area of recreation in which I had no interest for I was well aware that drugs had criminal implications.

In the street outside the Glenlyn, Mod boys would park their scooters and teenage girls anxiously surrounded their Vespas and Lambrettas to see which vehicle had the most lights, the biggest aerial, fox brush or the most chrome. I did have the occasional lift home clinging to the back of a 'fishtail' Parka, but had my parents known they would have despaired.

Another favourite venue for teenagers was the Bromley Court Hotel in Kent where popular bands performed, often within just a few feet of the audience. By day the relaxing lounges with their sumptuous sofas were used by paying guests. Then on Friday and Saturday nights the mood was replaced with the music of Georgie Fame and the Blue Flames. The Animals were regular acts, and during 1965/66 Long John Baldry and Rod Stewart, Brian Auger and Julie Driscoll performed together as Steampacket. How my friends and I got to the Orchid Ballroom in Purley in the mid-Sixties to see such pop groups I have no idea, but we managed to do so until the entrance fee increased to 7/6d, thus exceeding our disposable incomes.

Music at this time had become the most vital form

of communication for young people, whereas previously the young had been influenced by the movies and the ubiquitous stars crossing the Atlantic from the film studios in Hollywood.

So I bore witness to both the rewards and perils of being young during an exciting, revolutionary and somewhat turbulent time of great social change. Everywhere the young were questioning authorities, corporations and the establishment in general, and because I was a 1960s teenager my parents feared I might bring shame to their doorstep.

Indeed, on one occasion I did stay out all night at a party in west London and on my return home the next morning I had to face the wrath of my mother; beaten with a wooden coathanger and being grounded for a week was sufficient punishment to ever repeat such similar conduct.

My sister Brenda had by now left mother and I in Bermondsey in order to marry a police officer who had come from Somerset to London around 1954, aged sixteen, to join the police Cadet Service, then after Hendon training school he had been posted to the streets of Bermondsey where they happened to meet. At the time I knew of no-one else who was a police officer, so whenever mother and I visited Brenda and John in their marital home in Brockley, I took the opportunity of asking my brother-in-law about his work.

'Is it exciting being a Policeman in London?'

'Sometimes,' would be his only reply.

'What do you do?'

'This and that.'

The secrecy only served to fuel my curiosity further.

But it was on Friday 12th August 1966, during the

Middle Class Suburbia

school summer holidays, when I heard some devastating news being reported on the early evening news:

'Earlier today, the three man crew of Foxtrot 11, an unmarked police-Q-car from Shepherd's Bush Police Station, has been cold-bloodedly murdered near Wormwood Scrubs prison.'

Something like this had very rarely happened in the Metropolitan Police or any force within the UK. Villains didn't generally carry guns, and it was unthinkable to shoot dead three police officers.

This terrible incident, one of the most traumatic murder cases in London, was a turning point in my life and I knew exactly what I wanted to do.

Sydenham Police Station happened to be directly opposite my school in Dartmouth Road, so one afternoon I dared to venture inside.

I was received by a surly military-styled Sergeant who was standing behind the solid oak front desk. To him I boldly announced, 'I would like an application form to join the Metropolitan Police.'

With a wry smile the Sergeant handed the paperwork to a skinny, barely five foot four eighteen-year-old. Despite his attitude I was determined to fill out the application and once completed and posted I desperately hoped I would get a positive response. I had not consulted my parents nor my brother-in-law about this career choice and had no idea how they would react, but in the meantime I continued my part-time job in the chemist shop and returned to school in September of that year.

Around this time I lost my virginity to a boy who was one of a group of teenagers with whom my schoolfriends and I used to frequent. We would gather in a local coffee bar known as the Alpine in Forest Hill or in the

Criterion ice cream parlour in Sydenham. There was also Blackheath Common, a favourite meeting place where we would laze around on the grass in the summertime to do very little except listen to pop music on one of the groups' portable transistor radio.

Melvyn was a year older than me, needless to say a Mod, tall and devilishly attractive. His teeth were pearly white, with a Terry-Thomas gap in the front. He lived in New Cross in part of a depressed Victorian three-storey terrace with his mother and father. To spend time with him there I either had to take a train from Forest Hill or a bus to St John's Station. My mother didn't agree with the relationship because I was reluctant to tell her anything about who I was actually going out with, so sometimes for a few hours I recruited close girlfriends to act as alibis. As it happened Melvyn had been my only teenage crush, but when I told him I was thinking of joining the police his interest in me waned, especially as he had once been retained at Her Majesty's Pleasure in a boys' Borstal.

1966
Career Path

Whilst I awaited a response to my application, I did some research in my school library in order to find out about the history of women in the police force and discovered that a woman had held the office of Parish Constable during the reign of Queen Elizabeth but, being attached to property she owned, her duties may have been performed by a male proxy. For according to the Magna Carta, all men and youths of twelve years of age and above could be required to act as constable 'for the preservation of the King's peace and for the pursuit of felons by 'hue and cry', powers which can still be exercised by any person at common law.

Then, with the passage of time, paid 'Watches' were employed in cities, and in rural areas Parish constables were appointed. But it was during the Nineteenth century that Elizabeth Fry, the prison reformer, secured the first appointments of women as matrons in women's prisons, and other reformers gained entry into Magistrates' Courts as forerunners of the modern Probation Service.

Eventually, following women's efforts in WWI, in February 1919 women police patrols were appointed to the Metropolitan force. However, they would not be granted powers of arrest in line with their male colleagues until April 1923.

About a month after I had sent off my application to Scotland Yard I received an invitation to attend police premises at Borough High Street, just south of the Thames, for the interview process.

I accepted Douglas' offer to take me as I had no idea how to get there, and especially not by 8.30 in the morning. He drove me in his beloved Austin Cambridge, which he had bought new. From a limited selection of letters and numbers he chose DXD690 as the registration plate: 'D' for his initial, and '69' because every evening after dinner he would take a glass of Vat 69 whisky; the number plate was therefore as personalised as he could make it.

After a straightforward journey I was dropped off at the front door of the building with plenty of time to spare. As I was about to walk away Douglas called, 'Good luck.' That, from a man who rarely displayed any emotion, was unprecedented.

In the entrance hall I was met by a serious looking uniformed woman police officer.

'Name?' she bellowed before scanning the alphabetical list with her pen. 'Take the stairs to the first floor and wait there with the other hopefuls.'

I noticed there were no male applicants anywhere in the building, but soon discovered that their interviews were scheduled on different days from those of the women.

In the waiting area I sat down next to a very smart woman who appeared to be a little older than myself. She wore a pale blue Crimplene straight skirt to her knees and fitted jacket with a scalloped edge. Her short strawberry blonde bouffant hair would have resisted any gale.

As I waited I scanned the other women. I counted

eighteen dressed in smart interview attire, but in spite of their outward appearance they were all probably as nervous as myself, having not really prepared myself for what was involved. All I knew was the interview process was going to take most of that day.

Suddenly the smart woman next to me gave me a nudge.

'Hello pet, me name's Carol.'

The strange sounding introduction startled me. I had never heard of anything being called 'Pet' before, except my Pekingese Khandi, and of course my hamster.

'Hello,' I replied, 'where are you from?'

'I've come down here from Wallsend,' she informed me, 'near Newcastle-on-Tyne.'

I wasn't much the wiser. I knew the south west and the Cotswolds, and south London, but little else. Nevertheless, within a few minutes Carol chatted to me although I had to listen very carefully in order to decipher her accent. We sat together until the first stage of proceedings, the medical examination. Carol was called before I was, but as my surname started with 'W', I had to wait a while longer.

'Willoughby,' a nurse eventually called, handing me an oversized pink dressing gown. 'Strip to your underclothes and put this on.'

When she checked my height I took a deep breath and stretched upwards, gaining the extra half an inch needed for the minimum requirement of 5 feet 4 inches. In fact I was pleasantly surprised to be measured as 5 feet 4, and a half! This was then followed by an eye test and a cursory dental check. Finally, I was ushered into a large oak-panelled room where the Chief Medical Officer sat some distance away behind a polished oak desk.

'Have you got any ailments you wish to disclose?' he asked. The two fractures, tibia and skull incurred as an eleven-year-old after running in front of a speeding car in Ilderton Road, Bermondsey on the way home from school, a close encounter with my maker, did not present me with any problems so I chose not to disclose them.

'Touch your toes,' the CMO demanded frostily, 'without bending your knees.'

I was eighteen-years-old and could have stood on my head if he'd asked. Anyway, without further ado he bellowed, 'Get dressed.' followed by, 'Next!'

Although I didn't particularly like tea, at various intervals during the day copious paper cups of the muddy liquid were offered and I began to think drinking tea whether you liked it or not had to be a prerequisite of being a police officer. So drink it I did.

For the next part of the proceedings I was called before an interview panel consisting of four senior police officers, one Superintendent, two Inspectors, both male, and Mrs Shirley Becke, the woman Chief Superintendent in charge of A4 branch. Within the next three years she would become the Met's first woman Commander.

One of the Inspectors on the panel was younger and less intimidating than the others, so I began to feel a little more at ease.

'Why exactly do you want to be a police officer?'

I had not eaten since a very early breakfast and therefore feared my stomach would rumble noisily over my timid reply.

'Sir', I had to remember to be very respectful, 'My brother-in-law is a police officer at West End Central, and his work has always intrigued me.'

I knew if I was a successful candidate I would have to

do two years' probation before I could go on to anything like he did, but I was very keen to be part of a world beyond anything I had experienced before.

'What is his name?'

'John Summers, Sir.'

John was working on the Vice Squad at the time. And as luck would have it the younger Inspector, the one with a wide smile and twinkly eyes, was John's senior officer. Not what you know but who you know came to mind.

In due course, I was asked several further questions.

'What are your hobbies?'

"I enjoy Art and foreign travel.'

I went on to explain that I had visited most of Europe and had lived in Spain for a while as a child.

'What duties do you think a woman police officer has to perform?'

I responded by explaining a little, which wasn't much, but I did know there would be a great deal more to discover about police work in general if I was to be a successful applicant. I was desperate for success and my responses seemed to impress the panel.

But then Mrs Becke peered over her spectacles. 'You are a modern young woman. What are your views on the proposed new uniform for women police?'

Before entering the interview room I had been advised by the WPC overseeing the interviews to address a female officer above the rank of Sergeant as 'Ma'am', so after doing just that I responded:

'I rather like the current uniform, but in today's society there is a need for it to be practical rather than merely a fashion statement.'

Little did I know that Norman Hartnell was the designer who had already been chosen to design what was to become the most impractical uniform ever worn by the Metropolitan women police.

One final question was put to me to assess my political leanings: 'And what daily newspaper do you read?'

'*The Times*,' was my knee-jerk response. I thought that was a very adult answer and it seemed to be an acceptable one. But thankfully I was not asked any questions about a newspaper in which actually I had little interest; *The Daily Mail* was the tabloid that Douglas had delivered daily to our house. Thankfully the interrogation was over within the hour and Mrs Becke concluded, 'No more questions.'

After my interview, the lunch in the establishment's canteen was most welcome, even if it did have the aroma and familiarity of school dinners.

In the afternoon, every applicant had to sit to take a written test. As I understood it at the time, there was no difference made in regard to educational standards between women and men candidates. Most had reached a reasonable standard of education, and one or two could have had university degrees.

As a recent school leaver I was an exception as it turned out, as the other female candidates had teaching, social work, nursing, the armed forces or clerical experience to draw upon.

I did not have a GCE in either English Language or Mathematics, having only achieved passes in English Literature and A Level Art at school, so I had to answer questions on Maths and English, plus General Knowledge and Geography. But the question 'Why do young people tend to move from villages into towns when they grow up?' does, on reflection, seem a very dated discursive piece.

Career Path

Members of police selection boards seemingly felt that although there needed to be a minimum standard of education set by the entrance examination, the vital, necessary, qualities for recruits depended most of all upon temperament, experience and a personality 'likely to inspire and maintain confidence and respect in all encounters with members of the public'.

It was an arduous albeit interesting process, and I was glad when it was all over, although I sincerely hoped my answers and the way I had conducted myself at interview was sufficiently convincing for the panel to accept me.

The final part of the day was for each candidate to go to nearby St Thomas's Hospital for a chest X-ray.

A couple of weeks after the interview, as a matter of procedure, a local uniformed WPC called at my address to make enquiries about where and with whom I lived. I could not have been more middle class if I tried, probably the type of women the police force was looking for at the time.

Then about a month later the eagerly-awaited self-addressed buff-coloured envelope dropped through the letterbox onto the hall carpet.

'Mum, I've been accepted!'

1967

She's Leaving Home

I left home on 20th February 1967.

By now, mother and Douglas had resigned themselves to my chosen career path so delivered me to Peto House at 26 Aybrook Street in Marylebone, a Section House for women police in training. It was named after Dorothy Olivia Georgiana Peto, a pioneer of women policing in the United Kingdom. She served as the first attested female Superintendent in the Metropolitan police from 1930 to 1946.

During our final embrace my mother cried, 'We'll miss you, but I am so proud, The last nineteen years have been a roller coaster for us both but I know you are more than ready to embark on your next amazing adventure.' Douglas shook my hand with a smile and silently turned away.

Perhaps my birth sign was meant to determine my future: a perfect career choice for an Aquarian is one that provides a fair bit of flexibility and the opportunity to work for a good cause.

Or was it that I had come to realise my chaotic past unwittingly provided the perfect foundation for my chosen career?

I was raring to go.

1967

Peto House

On arrival in Peto House realisation dawned that this was to be my home for the next thirteen weeks. I was beginning to wonder what I had let myself in for, especially as the correspondence I had received prior to my arrival provided few details about the world I was to inhabit.

I was soon to find out, especially when I came face to face with the Warden, a florid faced woman with a broad Scottish accent that matched her dour demeanour; a seemingly necessary requirement for someone in charge of such an establishment. I was later told that prior to her becoming the Section House Sergeant she had been a Constable at Croydon Police Station, Z Division, and would have been made up to Sergeant on transfer to Peto House.

When women were first accepted into the Metropolitan Police they had to be between 25 and 38 years of age. Then in 1948 the lower age limit was reduced to 20, and again in 1962 to 19. Miss McNab definitely looked upon bright-eyed, bushy-tailed teenagers with much disdain; after all, we weren't even old enough to vote, but ironically we were about to take on the huge responsibility of upholding the law.

'I am Sergeant McNab.' Her large bosom expanded as she announced herself.

'There are rules here which have to be adhered to. Any failure to do so may result in a recruit being removed from the course and sent home forthwith. Do you understand?'

'Yes Miss, Sergeant I mean.'

A shaky initial introduction, but I resigned myself to the fact that I was about to enter a very adult environment and a career where rules were not to be broken. If they were, one would definitely have to face the consequences.

McNab went on to describe the layout of the three-storey house, much of which went over my head like it does when one is introduced to people at a party; only a few names actually sink in.

'Recruits here either have their own room, share a double or in some cases a larger three-bedded room.'

I did absorb that which affected me directly, so listened carefully.

'Your room is the one at the top of the hooss, and what's more be sure to be doon for dinner at seven o'clock precisely.'

'Yes Sergeant.'

As I walked up the two flights of stone stairs I glanced through the open doors of other bedrooms and saw that they were just big enough to house a single bed, a wardrobe and a wooden table and chair.

When I reached the top floor I entered my allocated room which was as spartan as the others, but I saw that it was a twin-bedded room.

I landed my well-worn brown leather suitcase on the linoleum-covered floor with a thud, and then tested each of the iron-framed bedsteads; both of them supported an unrelenting mattress and were topped with a grey utility blanket with the black initials M.P. woven into the fabric.

I decided to choose the bed nearest the window for no other reason than the view from it stretched out over London rooftops towards the Post Office Tower, a view of London I had not seen before but knew the metropolis was somewhere I was soon going to find out a lot more about.

Then I began to make myself at home by unpacking my meagre possessions and hanging a couple of dresses, two skirts, two blouses and my winter coat in the narrow wardrobe. Basic toiletries I placed neatly on the table.

Suddenly I was startled by a voice behind me. 'Hello Pet, hoo ye gannin?'

I turned and to my surprise it was Carol standing in the doorway, the applicant I had met on the day of my interview in Borough High Street.

Judging by her tone of voice I ascertained that Carol had asked me how I was.

'Fine,' I replied, and added 'It's good to see a friendly face.'

'The old bat told us I was sharing a room but I never dreamt it would be you.'

Carol of course had also been given her instructions by the formidable Miss McNab so, to avoid upsetting her, Carol deposited her case on the other bed and we both hurried down to the basement for our evening meal.

The kitchen was a large room with a wooden refractory table in the centre with six or so chairs on either side. Three other recruits similar in age to Carol and I had arrived earlier in the day and were already seated at the table.

'Hello, I'm Mary, and this is Muriel and Linda.'

I wondered how Linda, who was petite and the quietest of us all, would ever live up to the role of a police officer.

Muriel, a tall, confident and very attractive blonde, told us to call her 'Mu'.

The five of us chatted over a meal of meat and two veg prepared by Mavis, a local woman employed as our cook, although all the recruits had to help at meal times by setting the table or washing up, while Sergeant McNab called out her orders as were necessary to keep us busy.

Before Mavis left for the night she would put a sliced white loaf on a side table.

'You can toast this for supper if you get peckish.' The bread looked far from appetising. My mother baked her own bread at home, so I would miss its delicious aroma along with other previously taken-for-granted home comforts.

That first night the narrow bed proved to be more uncomfortable than I had expected. The white cotton sheets had been secured with envelope corners and held me in a vice like grip, but I must have got some sleep as the first thing I knew was the shrill ring of my alarm clock and I started the day with eager anticipation. Every day throughout training, including Saturday mornings, all of us women recruits in Peto House, about 20 in all who were at different stages of training, would be expected to wake at 6.00am.

Whilst I prepared for the day I would listen to Tony Blackburn on Radio London.[4] My mother had given me

---

4   Radio London was an offshore commercial or 'Pirate' station that operated from a ship anchored in the North Sea, three-and-a-half miles out from Frinton-on-Sea on the Essex coast. The transmissions from there lasted from December 1964 to 14 August 1967, when it and the other Pirate station, Radio Caroline, were outlawed.

a transistor radio as a leaving present. She wasn't one for sentimentality, so presents other than for Christmas or birthdays were rarely received, but this small item proved to be very useful.

Then after a hurried breakfast a scheduled coach took us to Peel House, the Metropolitan police training school, in Regency Street, SW1.

1967
Peel House

Peel House was a mere three miles away and took no more than twenty minutes, from Aybrook Street in Marylebone via Marble Arch, Park Lane, Piccadilly, Constitution Hill and Birdcage Walk. Often as we neared Buckingham Palace our paths would cross with the Household Cavalry, soldiers renowned worldwide for being superbly turned out. There can be no more splendid sight than the Sovereign's Escort on horseback, polished armour glinting in the morning sunlight. Finally, our route took us along Horseferry Road and into Regency Street.

Peel House, an old Victorian building, was named after Sir Robert Peel, who in 1829 was the founder of the Metropolitan Police Force. Its interior was stark, in parts tiled white walls and in others the walls painted cream, punctuated by dark brown windows and doors. It was like going back to school, only light years away from the modern building I had moved on from. Cramped, badly lit, with all the comforts of a prison. Although recruits expected to be allowed expeditions to the outside world during training, I soon realised the pressures of study would mean that they would have to be kept to a minimum.

As well as a training school, Peel House doubled as a Section House for a good many male recruits. However, due to the large intake of men at the time, formerly civilians, ex-army or Police Cadets, there was another Met Police Training School with men-only accommodation at Hendon, a London suburb in the Borough of Barnet, which had opened in 1934.

Before training actually commenced, all recruits were allocated a pay and warrant number.

'You will be 2339.' I was informed. 'This number will stay with you for the whole of your police service. From this day forward it will never change.' This was the first day of the rest of my life.

The next process was for us all to have our fingerprints taken, and on seeing how it was done I began to get most excited about having, in the course of future police work, to take someone else's prints. To this day prints including my own remain on file at the Fingerprint Branch at New Scotland Yard.

After all the formalities, we were taken to join our allocated class members to take an oath of allegiance to the Queen:

> I ...., being appointed a Constable of the Metropolitan Police District, do solemnly, sincerely, and truly declare and affirm that I will well and truly serve our Sovereign Lady, Queen Elizabeth, in the office of a Constable and that I will act as a Constable for preserving the peace, and preventing robberies and other felonies, and apprehending offenders against the peace, and in all respects to the best of my skill and knowledge, discharge the duties of the said office faithfully and according to law.

Peel House

At Peel House, the female recruits were supervised by a woman police Sergeant Sylvia King. She was friendly and approachable and it was good to have an ally in what was above all a male-dominated profession.

'Now girls, you have to report to me daily,' she announced, and went on to explain a few of the house rules.

Most seemed reasonable enough, but I couldn't see the point of us girls only being able to go to the toilet in pairs. Was the place so difficult to find one's way around by oneself, or was it for our own safety? I never really worked it out, and furthermore we also had to be escorted by Sergeant King to the canteen for our cups of tea before the day's training began. Rumour had it that the tea was laced with bromide, but considering the raucous behaviour of male recruits, who would whistle 'Colonel Bogey' as we bevy of fresh female recruits promenaded through the hall in single file behind Miss King, I doubted its effectiveness. Some of us were still naïve teenagers, but after a few days our blushes diminished and we soon learnt to ignore what in the future would be considered sexual harassment.

Initially the women's training school syllabus would be the same as that of the men. So after having taken the oath, I and my fellow probationers were provided with an instruction book, to be forever known as the I.B., a weighty black volume of over forty six chapters and several appendices; in which there would be so much to learn.

'Read and inwardly digest the first two pages of your I.B. You will be tested on it tomorrow!' was our police sergeant instructor's first announcement.

So the 'Primary objectives', written by Sir Richard

A Girl in Blue

Mayne who in 1829 was appointed as a Justice of the Peace in charge of the Force, was one of the many word-perfect pieces to master. And these particular objectives I could still manage to recite many years later:

> The primary object of an efficient police is the prevention of crime: the next that of detection and punishment of offenders if crime is committed. To these ends all the efforts of police must be directed. The protection of life and property, the preservation of public tranquility, and the absence of crime, will alone prove whether those efforts have been successful and whether the objects for which the police were appointed have been attained.

When the first civilian police force in the world, the London Metropolitan police, marched out from New Scotland Yard in 1829, their uniform was based on the civilian dress of the day. Totally different working conditions existed in those early days and it was clearly laid down in the Instructions that the constable was to wear his uniform at all times and he was, therefore, on duty at all times. The difference between being on duty and being off duty was indicated by whether the armlet, worn on the left sleeve of the uniform tunic, was on or off. The first armlets were horizontally striped and only had a few rings, but by the time I joined they were alternate vertical stripes of dark blue and white. Change would come yet again when the armlet was discontinued altogether in 1972.

In training school, each class generally consisted of twenty male recruits, whereas mine had five women and fifteen men. From the start, routine and high standards were paramount, and at least once a day every class would have to practise drill in the small quadrant that served as a parade ground named Savile Row. Sergeant Blewitt, a tall stocky man with a severe haircut scarcely discernible as ginger took drill. He was an ex-Army Sergeant whose main aim was to terrify recruits, and the women were particular targets.

'Lofty' was a young but very tall recruit who often got chosen to demonstrate the art of marching to us all, but 'Left right, left right' didn't come easy for those of us who had never set foot on a parade ground in our lives. Sergeant Blewitt loved to shout a quote about marching that had been written in a Civil and Military gazette during the 1800s:

'It's an infinity of booted feet coming down and taking up with the exactness of a machine'. Do you understand?!'

It was a case of having to, along with taking turns to deliver the orders.

'You, Willoughby, take the class.'

'A TEN SHUN! By the left, QUICK MARCH!'

Much to my surprise, I had found a strident voice hidden within me and subsequently I became known as the class 'RSM' (Regimental Sergeant Major - a British Army term for a drill Sergeant). This new-found ability gained me some favour with the Sergeant. However, he was not amused if any of us caused the squad to topple into one another like a set of dominoes as I once, and only once, had the misfortune of doing.

After a hard day of study, our return coach journey to Peto often resulted in recruits testing one another on the various Acts and sections that needed to be learnt.

'What is the definition of common assault?'

'A common assault is one in which no wound or serious injury is inflicted. It is an offence under the Offences Against the Person Act, 1861, section 42.'

A Girl in Blue

'Yeah, but what about GBH?' someone else would pipe up. 'Grievous Bodily Harm?'

'Same Act different section. Anybody know which one?'

And although some smart Alec would shout out 'Section 18' detailed knowledge was needed in preparation for our daily tests and our final exams.

In contrast to the intensity of study some light relief was gained by communal singing on the coach and I soon became aware of bawdy music hall songs, although most of the lyrics were anything but original...

> Bless 'em all, Bless 'em all.
> The long and the short and the tall, Bless all the Sergeants and WPCs
> Bless all those Gov'ners and their blinkin sons,
> Cos' we're saying goodbye to 'em all.
> And back to their stations they crawl,
> You'll get no promotion this side of the ocean,
> So cheer up my lads bless 'em all.

And our variation of *Down by the Riverside:*

> Gonna lay down my I.B,
> Down by the riverside,
> Down by the riverside,
> Down by the riverside.
> Gonna lay down my I.B,
> Down by the riverside,
> Down by the riverside.

Chorus:

> I ain't go study law no more,
> I ain't go study law no more.

Peel House

I ain't go study law no more,
I ain't go study law no more.

Since everything the I.B. threw at us had to be learnt parrot-fashion, in Peto House voices chanting acts and sections echoed throughout the evening and into the night like some divine practice.

A couple of weeks into the course women recruits had a few hours respite when we were sent to Uniquip, a clothing manufacturer located at 10 Clerkenwell Green, to be measured for our dark blue uniform serge skirt and tunics.

Until the uniforms were ready we had to wear civilian clothes to Peel House. But in the meantime we were issued with six collarless white cotton shirts and their accompanying detachable collars. Douglas wore such shirts to work, so the process of attaching the collar to the shirt with two collar studs, one at the back and one at the front, was not totally alien to me. There were facilities in the section house for us to launder our own shirts, but in the same street as Peto House was a laundry where every week we took our detachable collars to be cleaned but although immaculate, the resulting stiffly starched collars positively chafed delicate necks.

Then there was the provision of three pairs of black, Pretty Polly seamed stockings. We treated them with kid gloves as one had to pay for any replacements before the next ones arrived. A navy blue gabardine mac, as well as a double-breasted woollen greatcoat, was issued for wear outside in inclement or severe weather conditions. Although a heavy garment, it was so incredibly smart and warm to wear.

Additionally, a wooden truncheon, shorter than the male PCs' version, was supplied to the women officers to be kept in a discreet pocket inside the uniform skirt. Pocket books for recording incidents and road traffic offences were kept in breast pockets and completed our 'appointments'.

The uniform my contemporaries and I wore was known as the 'Bather' uniform, as it had been devised by Elizabeth Bather, a police officer who served as the second Commander of the London Metropolitan Police's A4 Branch (women police) from 1946 to 1960. In 1949 she became the first female police officer in the United Kingdom to be promoted to the rank of Chief Superintendent. Bather attempted to 'feminise' the force, redesigning the uniform in 1946 and allowing policewomen to wear make-up on duty. In 1946 she also removed the bar on married women joining, and overturned the rule against serving policewomen getting married, a ruling which had been in force since the 1920s.

Police officers were provided with their uniform free of charge, and furthermore were made aware about the clothing van that would visit police stations every month or so to exchange or readily obtain various worn out or damaged items. Also officers were entitled to a monetary shoe allowance. My regulation flat black lace-ups, without embellishments or exaggerated shape, were purchased from a uniform source. They amused my mother no end as they were a far cry from the fashion shoes I normally wore. For inspection purposes, uniform black shoes had to be polished until the toecaps gleamed like glass. One day as I relaxed with other class members in the communal lounge between lectures, I sidled over to Rube, an ex-Marine. If he didn't know how to make leather gleam nobody would.

'Rube, how can I get my shoes as shiny as the men do?'

Peel House

'Young lady,' Rube was at least ten years older than I. 'It's a lengthy process. You take some black Kiwi polish on a yellow duster and apply the waxy paste in small circles on to the leather.'

I happened to have a tin of polish and a duster in my kit bag so was ready to learn how to improve my previous attempts.

Rube took the tin and proceeded to spit onto the black circle of wax inside and apply it to his boots. I was learning fast.

'That's why it's called 'spit and polish.''

'Oh, of course!'

'Another option is to melt some of the wax in a metal spoon over a candle flame before rubbing it into the leather,' Rube continued.

The latter I never attempted for fear of razing a police establishment to the ground.

But with the necessary advice gained, I sat bulling my toecaps for as long as it took before our next lecture and achieved the obligatory results, a process that I would repeat time and time again throughout my service.

As it was, every weekday around 8.30am each class of recruits had to assemble either in the main hall or outside on the quadrant parade ground for uniform inspection by one of the senior officers. It was essential to remain immaculate, even to the extent of threatening a colleague with near death if they came too close. An impeccable appearance was everything.

We recruits were also taught how to salute; a short right arm straight up from the elbow action, different from the salutes of the armed forces, having been devised to be used whilst on parade, in a confined space or when addressing a senior officer. But in fact the only time I

A Girl in Blue

did salute after training school was in the town centre in respect for a passing funeral cortege, yet this age-old tradition was not upheld by many and sadly diminished with time.

So in due course everyone in Peto House adjusted to their new lives and routines. The communal lounge contained a couple of sofas and a television although none of us had the time for watching it due to being too busy or too tired. Close relatives were only allowed to visit by appointment those recruits who were unable to get home. Those of us who lived within the Metropolitan police district were permitted leave of absence for a day and half from midday on Saturday until Sunday night and most weekends I took advantage of a few hours of freedom.

At 10.00pm every night, the doors of Peto House were locked by Sgt McNab. However, one of the recruits who had been in the house a few weeks longer than the majority of us happened to share some very useful advice.

'If you open the front door ever so slightly you can squeeze through the gap without the alarm going off in Nab's office.'

This escape route was irresistibly tempting. So most of us took advantage of it, even though to do so could be perilous and anyone, at any time, who was late home or seen talking to friends outside on the pavement – especially with members of the opposite sex – would be strongly reprimanded and likely to be denied social leave altogether. One day when it was discovered that an unmarried woman recruit was pregnant she was subsequently cast out into the cold, never to return. Such was the wrath of McNab although she could be very supportive if any of us was homesick or ill.

Apart from those women who preferred same-sex partnerships, many female recruits were asked out by single PCs. During training school I dated Graham, an ex-cadet, also was also nineteen and in my class. The fact that he had a 'frog-eye' Austin-Healey Sprite was particularly appealing as I had never had a boyfriend with a car let alone a sports model, so riding around London in it was exhilarating.

Our social life consisted mainly of meeting up with friends in one of the pubs near training school. A favourite was the White Swan in Victoria, or the 'Mucky Duck' as it was known locally. Then there was also the Gunmaker pub a few doors down from Peto House. The most I ever allowed myself to drink socially was half a lager shandy for apart from the occasional small glass of red wine Douglas had introduced to me at home, I was not used to drinking and most recruits chose to abstain whilst in training.

On a few occasions, especially after we got engaged, somewhat hastily I might add, Graham took me to visit his family in Nottingham. They, the Shepherd family, were all from farming stock so having a son join the Police was not easy for them to accept nor was his not having taken a local lass as a fiancée.

'A Londoner eh? Before long she'll be the one wearing the trousers, you mark my words!' was his father's reaction to our liaison and his opinion of my developing air of confidence.

Training continued with a full timetable of lectures. Acts of Law had to be studied and either recited parrot fashion or included in answers posed in Knowledge & Reasoning essays set by the instructors. Then, as a whole class, we also had to take part in practical demonstrations

A Girl in Blue

outside in the yard. The instructors would set up roleplay situations, enabling them to show off their frustrated thespian skills by pretending to be a casualty, a drunk, a vagrant, a child, a whore, a thief or, sometimes, a policeman! All tasks were designed to prepare us for what we would have to deal with 'on the beat'. But one thing for sure was if an instructor decided he did not like a particular recruit, he or she would never forget it.

On arrival at a scene of an incident a police officer's duty was, before anything else, to attend to any injured party - 'the protection of life' - and thereafter, particularly at road accidents, try to ascertain if there were any witnesses. One had to shout as loudly as possible,

'DID ANYBODY SEE WHAT HAPPENED?!'

This demonstration of authority needed to be secure in preparation for its possible use in every day police work.

Then, during one particular mock incident I was dealing with the instructor suddenly stopped and shouted at me.

'Girl… what did you have for breakfast this morning? Bird seed?' His attempt to embarrass me nearly succeeded but I appreciated that I would have to speak more slowly if I was to acquire the necessary demeanour of a police officer in the outside world.

In another scenario, where I had to act out my first arrest, I started off by saying, 'Sir, I'm afraid I will have to arrest you.'

'AFRAID, OFFICER? AFRAID? I never want to hear you say you are AFRAID about anything! Do you hear me?'

'Yes Sarge, sorry Sarge.'

About halfway through the course the Superintendent in charge of Training School, a formidable man called Tommy Wall made an appearance. He was a large man;

over six feet tall and probably weighing twenty stone. His reputation had gone before him as he was especially known for his bullying tactics. Usually when he entered a classroom he would swear at any recruit who looked ever so slightly timorous.

To test a young WPC's mettle I once witnessed him attempt to undo the buttons on the front of her uniform shirt. She slapped his face hard.

Tommy responded, 'Good girl. That's what I was expecting!'

Superintendent Wall's actions conveyed a conflicting message to his audience that day. Provocation might have caused a civilian to assault another, but not a police officer. After all, an assault is, and was then, an arrestable offence. However, the message Tommy Wall was trying to convey was for an officer to be prepared for the unexpected. The strict regime of training, and the bizarre ways that recruits were put to task, definitely sorted the wheat from the chaff and some did fall along the way, as did the female whose shirt buttons were the focus of attention. She immediately put in her resignation and was gone in just a few hours.

Apart from being very sexist, (although he would say his approach was to toughen up female recruits) Superintendent Wall delivered a strong message to those who did make it through to the end of the thirteen weeks…

'At the end of your training, you will go out to a different world. None of you will ever leave this place and be embarrassed on the streets by what people say to you. You will see and do things that thirteen weeks ago you had never even heard about. You will cross the road to go to things thirteen weeks before you would have crossed the road to walk away from. Your life will change forever!'

Although women police constables had the same power of arrest and did the same job as their male colleagues, we had to be further trained for a specialist role regarding laws relating to women and children. So about once a fortnight, women recruits had extra training sessions in a room in the rear of Peto where we learnt about the Children and Young Persons Act of 1933.

Furthermore there was instruction about how to take rape statements, 'rape' then defined by the Sexual Offences Act, 1956, and how a WPC would need to assist those females who found themselves victims of such an offence. We had to learn the laws regarding infanticide, incest and abortion, the latter resounding heavily on my conscious as it was my sister Brenda who had told me about the time how as a young girl in Bexley she had assisted her mother with the abortion. When I first joined the police, abortion was still illegal under the Offences Against the Person Act, 1861 and was punishable with a term of imprisonment, but in 1967 an Act was passed in the UK to legalise it for women who were up to 24 weeks pregnant. Two consenting doctors had to agree that continuing the pregnancy would be harmful either physically or mentally for the mother, or the child after it was born. However, the act did not come into effect until 27 April 1968, so during my first year of service I had to be mindful of back street terminations.

There was also much instruction for us women recruits about the Street Offences Act of 1959, which later on in my career I would be dealing with first hand.

Although the course was already difficult enough, some four or five sessions of First Aid had to be attended. The

Peel House

instructor had the nickname 'Nuclear Ned', a tall, wiry police sergeant so called because part of the course he delivered was about how to deal with a possible nuclear attack during the Cold War. All the women in the class became wary of him.

'He's undressing us with his eyes.' Carol, being older and more experienced than any of us, would whisper. 'He's a bit of a letch.'

So at arm's length we'd try to stay, but nevertheless Ned would leer at any of us who appeared not to be paying attention.

'If any of you fail the First Aid exam you know you are out. Yes O-U-T out!' he would bellow. In spite of Ned, the First Aid sessions generally provided some light relief as we tussled with bandages, make-do splints and Resusci Annie, on whom we practiced mouth-to-mouth resuscitation. We only had to get half of the questions correct to pass, so I considered I had a fifty percent chance of becoming a police officer.

Regular PE sessions were timetabled in the sports hall at Hendon Police Training School and in order to get there recruits had to be transported by coach from Peel House, which took about forty minutes on a good run. Once there we did work-outs, running and step-ups, but the session also included defensive tactics, control and physical restraint instruction. I had previously belonged to a judo club at school, and although I never got further than a yellow belt I was keen to have the opportunity to improve my skills.

Every police officer is expected to be able to swim although I was never asked whether I could do so during my interview in Borough High Street. However, swimming lessons were part of the training so every fortnight recruits were timetabled to get themselves to the baths in Victoria.

There I declared I was a non-swimmer and the instructor did try to teach me, but his reaction said it all.

'Miss, if you can only swim in circles and most of the time with one foot on the bottom you are not going to get very far!'

Fortunately, or unfortunately for anyone who may have needed me to rescue them from the murky depths, the swimming instructor concentrated mainly on developing the lifesaving team and I was ignored.

Another aspect of our coursework was learning about Court procedures and we all had to take our turn to give evidence in mock-trials set up by belligerent instructors. Few recruits were natural orators, but we had to learn how to deal with being grilled by an instructor acting out the role of a defence lawyer. Throughout training school I discovered how fascinating the legal system is, from its very foundations to its increasingly important and visible role in virtually all areas of life, but giving evidence could be a terrifying experience, acted out in the main hall in front of half the personnel of training school. And as each recruit waited their turn to enter 'the box' to give evidence they would physically shake.

My turn came to present a 'Not Guilty' case of illegal gaming.

'Hold the book in your right hand and repeat after me,' droned the usher and I struggled through the Oath. 'I-I swear by almighty G-God ...' Deep breath,

'The evidence I shall give...'

I questioned my chances of uttering the next part of the Oath.

'Officer, is anything the matter?' The mock magistrate

Peel House

asked.

'No Sir.' I stuttered.

Although this was only a training exercise I could feel myself trembling with fear. It's not that I didn't have the evidence or the wherewithal to present my case, I merely couldn't stop shaking.

'Officer, I have a long list of cases this morning, will you please get on with it.'

I held on to the shelf of the witness box in which I was standing for stability, again took a deep breath and presented my case starting with day, date, time and place.

'Sir, I was on duty in uniform, when a member of the public reported illegal gaming.'

'What was the game?'

"Three-card trick sir.'

'Where was the accused working?'

'On the pavement outside a public house.'

'Under which Act was this an offence?'

'The Betting, Gaming and Lotteries Act 1963.'

'Good. Tell me more.'

'I approached the accused, cautioned him and took possession of the betting cards and the large quantity of money he had on him.'

'What did he say when you arrested him?'

'It's a fair cop Guv!'

A titter went round the other recruits who were watching, and I had to bite my tongue to suppress a fit of giggles. I could simply see the funny side of this charade, but by the end of my evidence I had somehow managed to persuade the Magistrate that an 'offence' had been committed, so the culprit was indeed found 'guilty'.

Court appearances never got any better during my

career, although I think that was much the same for most officers. However, the training held us in good stead for when we were faced with serious cross-examination in genuine cases later on in our service.

A couple of weeks before we were due to leave Peto House, we five women recruits had to move to a 'hostel for young ladies' in Pembridge Hall, Bayswater, as our rooms in Peto were needed for incoming recruits. Pembridge was a former Edwardian hotel, but the larger bedrooms had been sub-divided for single occupancy and the living rooms altered to serve as a dining area and common room for the 42 women that could be accommodated there. Women who were fully trained and working at west London police stations. We never returned to Peto House but heard it eventually closed in 1975, after 27 years accommodating women police recruits.

Then during our final week of training school our class had to attend Southwark Crown Court or Sessions as it was called at the time to listen to some of the cases on trial there that had been sent from Magistrates' courts.

We all had to be in civvies, the men in suits and the women in smart attire with obligatory hats. None of us had ever worn a hat for a formal occasion before, but we had great fun searching through a myriad of styles in West End departmental stores for them. We had been warned about needing a special outfit for this Court visit, so my mother took me to an exclusive dress shop in Regent Street to purchase a camel and green wool dress with matching coat. The hat I subsequently chose from Selfridges was a light-brown shiny raffia boater that I wore on the back of my head, and heeled leather shoes in a complimentary shade of brown completed the ensemble. Interestingly our group of women was the last one to have to wear hats for that foray.

Peel House

Following instruction on Court procedure, male recruits were taken to visit Pentonville prison while women recruits were taken to HM Prison Holloway (sometimes known as Holloway Castle), a closed-category prison for adult women and young offenders in north London. Many infamous women had been incarcerated within its walls, so entering the prison through its grand turreted gateway was especially daunting, although more so was the couple of minutes I was locked in one of the padded cells by one of the prison guard guides.

Most evenings, recruits could be found studying and revising for the crucial final examination. If we failed we would be put back a week or so to re-study. Not all the recruits managed to pass the final exams, and some didn't even get that far. For various reasons, either personal or academic, the training to become a police officer was not for them, and one man in my intake even got arrested for gross indecency, which swiftly ended his planned career path.

Another incident that became the talk of the whole school was when a young male recruit returned to Peel House some hours after the ten o'clock curfew. Even Cinderella had two hours longer. Because the front doors were locked, he decided to climb over the railings into the yard but fell and impaled himself on one of the spikes. Fortunately his injuries were not life threatening, but he was unable to sit down for several days. After receiving a severe reprimand from the Superintendent he was very lucky to be allowed to continue on the course.

Towards the end of our course each of us were sent to a London police station in uniform to experience a day in the life of a fully-fledged Constable. I was sent to Walworth Road, where WPC Evans and I patrolled the first under-cover shopping mall in Europe at nearby

Elephant and Castle.

'This shopping centre has only been opened a couple of years.' WPC Evans informed me. 'But apart from the occasional shoplifter, police here mainly deal with people who sleep in the shop doorways.'

'What, under the Vagrancy Act, Section 4, 1824?' I enjoyed airing my new-found knowledge.

'That's the one.'

'Tell me more.'

'Any homeless or destitute persons we pick up will be directed to a suitable shelter. There's a list on the wall in the nick of the charitable institutions we can send them to, depending on their age, sex and class.'

I spotted an unkempt old lady, bent over and carrying a bundle of meagre possessions.

'That's Nelly,' the WPC explained, 'poor old thing, homeless most of the time. She's lived on this manor all her life. Probably knew Charlie Chaplin.'

'What would you do with Nelly? Would you arrest her?'

'No, but she would like us to so she could get a bed for the night and a meal in the morning.'

Back at the police station I had a tour of the various departments and in the front office I noticed a list of charitable institutions in London which people like Nelly would be taken to by police, more often than not, a WPC. In the women police office I was shown day-to-day incident books, reports and details of missing person enquiries which demonstrated to me early on that a police officer was paid not for what they did, but for what they might have to do.

The majority of us were very relieved when we got to the end of the thirteen weeks and had passed our exams.

Peel House

Then I and several other successful female recruits were sent to New Scotland Yard, then at 4 Whitehall Place, to be congratulated by Mrs Becke in her office. There each of us was given our warrant card, an unimpressive black folded cardboard authorisation signed by the Commissioner of the Metropolis.

However, as soon as I became a police officer, being in possession of a Metropolitan Police Warrant Card was like having a passport to Nirvana. Flashing the card enabled its holder to gain access to everywhere and anywhere, unless a warrant was required to do so. Free transport throughout London on buses, tubes and trains was also permitted. Entry fees to public places such as museums, cinemas and exhibitions would be waived, on the assumption that police were investigating a case or were following a suspect.

After the formalities were over, an end of course dance in Peel House provided much needed light relief from the intensity of training. Afterwards, Mu and I were escorted back to Pembridge Hall by a couple of male friends who intended to carry on with the festivities back inside the house. But as usual their plans were thwarted by the warden there, who did not allow men, then or ever, to get past the front door!

At the end of training school successful recruits were given a week's leave. During that time, Douglas and my mother took Graham and me out for a special celebratory dinner in Patrick Gwynne's iconic Serpentine Restaurant on the eastern edge of Hyde Park.

It was such a relief for training to be over but following our leave we all had to report back to Peel House to find out which division and station we were to be posted. It was hoped that at least one of our divisional preferences, submitted by each of us at the end of training school, would be considered. The Training School Superintendent (not Tommy Wall, as he died suddenly towards the end of our course) took the passing out parade. But before we were told our fate, he reminded us of the principles of Sir Robert Peel:

> The police are the public and the public are the police; the police being only members of the public who are paid to give full time attention to duties which are incumbent on every citizen in the interests of community welfare and existence.

The passage served to remind us rooky cops what we had signed up for and what we should consider as we left the school. Then each of us was approached.

'You, WPC Willoughby, are going to K Division.'

'Pardon, Sir? I tried to sound respectful, but my heart sank at the news. It was most disconcerting to find myself being posted not the C Division where I had so wanted to work, but to K Division of all places!

The Superintendent looked at me wearily and repeated, 'Romford!'

I had a vague idea that Romford was in Essex and dared to ask for further details, 'Sir, where's Romford?'

'You'll find out.'

Carol was next in line, and much to my surprise she too was told she was going to Romford. I suppose that was some consolation, but the news was received with some disappointment as Carol knew even less about Romford than I did. We had both expected to be working in the bright lights of the West End rather than the flat lands of Essex, but for the time being nothing could be done, so we had to accept our fate.

To be sent to the very eastern edge of the metropolis to somewhere as unfamiliar as Romford was one thing, but it also meant that Carol and I would be in less than easy reach of our boyfriends. Graham was posted to Shepherds Bush, F Division in south west London, and Carol's boyfriend Ken, whom she had also met in training school, was posted to a north London police station. Neither Carol nor I had our own transport so our long distance relationships would be tested.

Next in line was Muriel. From my first day in Peto House Muriel intrigued me, having never met anyone quite like her before. She was an irrepressible platinum blonde, all fully-fashioned nylons and red lipstick. She loved to go out in the evenings, smoked cigarettes and was a bit of a flirt, ready to go out with any of the single PCs who asked her, and given half the chance liked to set up blind dates for her friends. Over a supper of toast and jam in the basement kitchen I had asked Muriel about herself.

'What did you do before applying for the Job Mu?'

'I was in the army for a couple of years. Married a soldier but that all went wrong, so I thought I could do no worse than to become a copper.'

'You single now?'

'Yeah, got my decree nisi just before my interview so then I knew I had a clear path ahead to a new career.'

Her destiny was Shooter's Hill police Station, R Division. She had never been south of the Thames, but the pattern of 'you're not going to be sent anywhere that you are familiar with' was set. Mary Bailey's posting was no different and she was sent to Kennington, M Division in Lambeth. However, true to my earlier assumptions, Linda never completed the course and left halfway through, and I completely lost touch with her.

Muriel mostly moved around R Division but at one time she was attached to the Accident Prevention Unit and became one of the first five women police to have a vehicle examiner's 'ticket', as it was known, and enjoyed the work until equality was introduced in 1973. That year without little backup she had to deal with a nasty pub brawl in Belvedere. Equality was not what she wanted, and so she decided to look once again for another career.

1967
Posted to the Sticks

The account of my police training is much the same as that of any other woman who went through the system at the time, but thereafter every woman police constable's experience would be shaped according to where she was sent to work. Some women would be called upon to do less than others and some more, but I can only describe the journey I travelled upon whilst serving in the Metropolitan Police Force.

From the outset, although I was only nineteen, I knew I was well prepared for the tasks ahead. My end of training school exam result was good and it was perhaps advantageous that I was a product of a dysfunctional family, having witnessed upset, loss, abuse and isolation and was aware of the struggles and temptations young people could face.

So it was in June 1967 that Carol and I were transported in a police utility coach to Romford, an Essex market town, about sixteen miles from the centre of London. On our arrival, we found it so different from the hustle and bustle of the city. Romford police Station, known as KD (Kilo Delta), had been built two years previously in a pleasant, tree-lined road. It was built to replace a large Victorian brick building in South Street, formerly part of the Essex Constabulary until it was swallowed up by the Metropolitan Police District in 1965.

Adjacent to Romford police station stood the equally newly-built courthouse. The two buildings gave the impression of sensible and sturdy planning, but generally the public were unaware that there was a connecting underground tunnel through which prisoners were conveyed.

Carol and I announced ourselves to the Station Sergeant on the front desk and he ushered us into the office of woman Sergeant Edith Cross, who was to be our mentor. She let us deposit our luggage in the women police office adjacent to hers, and then took us upstairs to be introduced to the Chief Superintendent. The station was busy, and en-route to his office policemen were going about their business, some rushing past, others coming or going with cups of tea or sheets of correspondence.

'Sir, these are my two new WPCs. WPC Hood and WPC Willoughby'.

It was clear from her possessive, curt introduction that she would clearly want to take us under her wing as would a mother hen, but I was not sure I liked the idea since I had joined the police to distance myself from my mother's apron strings, not reattach myself to someone else's.

The Governor sat behind a very well-ordered desk and looked up as we entered.

'Welcome to Romford, ladies. I hope you are ready for your work here?'

'Yes, Sir.' Carol and I replied in unison.

'Sergeant Cross will tell you your duties and I look forward to hearing how you are getting along.'

Then without further ado Carol and I were able to

return to the women police office which overlooked the station yard. We heard a lot of shouting going on and saw two officers struggling to get an aggressive male through the charge room door. Carol and I looked at one another and I said, 'This now is for real.'

To complete our uniform of blue serge, white shirt and black tie and shiny peaked cap, Carol and I were presented with a whistle and chain with a key attached for opening police boxes to attach to our jacket. At training school, only our appointed class captain had been given the honour of a whistle and chain accessory in order to differentiate him from the rest of us.

Finally, Carol and I were allocated our collar numbers, so called as historically numbers were attached to the collars of both men and women officers' high-necked tunics. But when shirts became part of the uniform the numbers were attached to the shoulder epaulettes. I became WPC 80K, which in itself was unusual as Constables were normally given three numerals and a letter. At the time I gave this little thought, other than I knew two numbers were usually supplied to a police officer who had reached the rank of Sergeant.

Before long, Carol and I discovered that the majority of officers with whom we would be working alongside were married men. Some had chosen to transfer from the Essex Constabulary when it was taken over by the Met, while others had taken the opportunity to increase the necessary manpower by transferring from central London with their families to a house in Havering's greener pastures.

So we had to accept the fact that our social lives would probably be less exciting than expected, but for the time being we were ready to face the next chapter of our lives.

A Girl in Blue

On my first proper day of duty I discovered women officers did not have to parade with their male colleagues in the parade room, so I reported to Sergeant Cross for a short briefing. Then it was a matter of checking the women police handover book to see what ongoing enquiries had to be dealt with or what reports needed to be written. Also in the front office there was the regularly updated volume of Police Orders circulated by Scotland Yard to be read which contained confidential information about all sorts of police matters. Afterwards Sergeant Cross asked a regular WPC to take me to the canteen, where I could get to know some of the other K Division officers.

There some of the PCs were engaged in a game of snooker and others were sitting at tables writing up their notes in pocketbooks.

My escorting WPC, Doreen, was usually employed at Harold Hill Police Station but she had been brought over to Romford for the day. We lined up at the counter and I met Babs, the canteen manager, who was busy cooking breakfasts for some of the Early Turn relief. Doreen and I were served tea, in 'Beryl' china cups.

I suddenly felt far greener than the cup I gripped in my hands, not wanting to let anyone see that I was feeling somewhat self-conscious in these unfamiliar surroundings.

One of the PCs leaned across from the other end of the table. 'Your mate isn't saying much.'

'It's her first day,' said Doreen defensively.

'Can she talk?'

I felt my face flush. I didn't have a clue what to say so continued drinking the dark brown liquid.

'She's got a lot to learn.' The PC echoed his remark

around the spacious interior, while I turned and looked out to the street through the wall of glass beside me.

Just then a uniformed officer sat down beside Doreen. He was about 26-years-old and tall - taller than the required 5' 8". He had a full head of white blonde hair and a fresh complexion.

'Hello, I'm Tony. Introduce me to your new colleague, Dor.'

'WPC 80K Willoughby.'

'Sarge,' I nodded at him respectfully.

'Now don't look so worried, you'll soon settle down. Just a few things you should know about this place.'

I was hungry for any information he could offer.

'You can call me 'Skipper', but keep to 'Sergeant' if there's any brass around, but in time you should be ok with 'Guv' for the Inspectors - apart from the women that is!'

'Right.'

'Have you had a look at the cars in the yard?'

'No, not yet but I'd like to.'

'Well all in good time. But listen up while I've got time to tell you. If I suddenly jump up and leave though, it's 'cos there's been a shout. Anyway, Station vehicles are called by the divisional letter and a number. 'Kilo 7' is the fast response area car, a Jag, J4 is the van, radio transmitters are RTs and Constables are generally referred to by number and not name, and a 'Q' car is the unmarked vehicle used by CID officers.'

Sergeant Cross had not imparted any of this information to me, so I listened intently.

'Oh, and the motley crew of blokes you see in civvies around the nick are in the CID. There's one over there.'

Wry smiles were exchanged between the Sergeant and the young good-looking detective sitting at one of the tables reading the *Romford Recorder*.

Maybe I might work with him one day I pondered, but my attention was suddenly diverted when I heard someone shout, 'There's been an attempted robbery at Lloyds' Bank in the Market Place!'

All the uniform officers, including Tony, rushed out of the canteen and flew down the stairs.

Teas, coffees, plates of food were abandoned but DC 'Didn't-know-his-name' remained in place. Neither Doreen nor I had to join the others, so we sat and chatted a while until we were joined by Sergeant Cross.

'Gels, we've had two local teenagers reported missing from their home addresses.'

Sergeant Cross added more details: names, addresses, dates of birth.

'The parents checked out school and neither of them went there today.'

'Are any boyfriends involved?' Doreen asked.

'Apparently they have both been seeing undesirable lads, a bit older than them, parents think this is the best lead to follow.'

Further details and descriptions were given to Doreen and in the women police office she telephoned the A4 Branch at New Scotland Yard, where since 1930 all records of children and young persons coming to the attention of the police were kept.

After a short conversation with a WPC at the yard, Doreen announced:

'One of the girls was stopped a few weeks ago in Romford in the company of Fred Tweedie, who works in the coalyard beside Romford train station. I think we should look there first.'

So Doreen and I got to the coal yard just before it closed and spoke to the foreman.

'Have you seen Fred Tweedie today?'

'He was in work this morning but took the afternoon off.'

'Did you see him leave?'

'Yes, with a couple of youngsters.'

'Girls?'

'Yes'

'Which way did they go?'

'Didn't really see. Another bloke joined them and they just vanished.'

'Would you have seen them go out into South Street if they had done so?

'Yes, from my office I can see into the coal yard and the street.'

Looking at me, Doreen said, 'In that case we need to search the yard.'

All I could think of was my pristine uniform and shiny shoes and I was about to climb in and out of coal trucks!

It was a sunny, late Friday afternoon in June. I could see people alighting trains on the railway station platform nearby, hurrying to get home to unwind or stopping off to have a quick drink in the pub across the road.

Then the foreman let Doreen and I into the yard and to the start of a line of stationary coal trucks filled with shiny black lumps of cargo.

As we walked beside the track we called out the names of the girls, whom we hoped we had a good chance of finding and banged on the side of each truck with our truncheons.

A Girl in Blue

After about ten trucks, none of which revealed any signs of life, we came to a truck in which we could hear giggling. Doreen gave me a shove up the side of the truck. I climbed stealthily, not wanting to alert anyone inside, but made myself known as I appeared over the side of the empty vessel; empty except for four teenagers, two of whom answered the girls' description.

I shouted to one of the boys. 'Are you Fred Tweedie?'

'Who wants to know?'

'Police.'

With that the two girls jumped up, stamped out the cigarettes they had been smoking onto the coal dust floor of the truck and looked very sheepish.

'They are all in here' I called down to Doreen, who was still holding my ankles.

Suddenly two PCs appeared out of nowhere, seemingly alerted by the coalyard foreman who was concerned for the safety of us 'lady policemen'.

'Get out girls, you need to go home,' I demanded. 'What were you planning to do? Run away in a coal truck or what?'

'Me and the other three,' said one of the girls, 'were going to go up the tracks further when it got dark, to a disused maintenance carriage. Fred said for an all-nighter.'

The PCs confirmed that the boys were over eighteen, and since the girls had come to no harm on this occasion they were taken home, given a severe warning and handed over to relieved parents. The details of both girls were put on record at A4 Branch and my work at KD had begun.

My eagerly-awaited starting salary at age nineteen was to be £710 per annum, ninety percent of that awarded to male constables. This was handed out weekly by Sergeant

Cross in a small brown envelope containing £13 cash. This routine was followed until I opened a building society account to enable me to save some of this vast income! But of course this was all relative to the time.

Women police worked seven and half hour shifts of alternate weeks of early and late turns, then one week of nights, whereas the daily shift for male officers was eight hours and night duty was a continuous three weeks, so the ten percent difference in pay was somewhat acceptable.

Police officers of any rank did not have to pay for their accommodation, and one of the incentives that enticed married men to join the Force was rent aid. Other inducements were clothing, travel and refreshment allowances. Rent aid went towards renting private accommodation or a mortgage. Single probationers, those who had not yet completed two years' service, were required in the sixties to live in one of Section Houses within the Metropolitan Police district. Such accommodation was provided in lieu of rent aid. As far as Carol and I were concerned, we were to reside at 312 St Mary's Lane in Upminster, in a part of the police station premises - a place we hoped would be more convivial than the barrack-style Section Houses.

When we arrived, Beryl, another Romford WPC, was in the house.

'Welcome to Upminster,' she greeted us in her non-Essex accent.

'So you're another immigrant?' I asked.

'Got it in one. Derbyshire, born and bred on a farm.'

'What brought you down south?'

'Wanted to police the bright lights of London. Look where that got me.'

'Us too,' said Carol.

As Beryl was showing us around I asked her, 'How long have you lived here?'

'Since the takeover; part of the nick next door was converted for the proposed increase of women police to the Borough.'

'A couple of years then?'

'Yep.'

There were three bedrooms, two upstairs and one down. Carol and I had to share the double one overlooking St Mary's Lane. The house was well-appointed although somewhat dated, seemingly furnished with a few secondhand pieces of furniture, but this was to be our new home.

Carol and I doubled the previous quota of two policewomen stationed at Romford, covering Romford sub-division, although there were occasions when there might be only one WPC covering the whole division.

Since the four women officers would all be on different shift patterns we rarely saw one another, as one of us would be on lates, the other earlies, the other night duty, generally only meeting up in the house if one of us was on leave, but at least there was rarely a queue for the bathroom, a starkly-appointed white-tiled extension to the house.

A similar women police hostel was situated above Barking Police Station, which provided accommodation for half-a-dozen women officers attached to any of the other K sub-division police stations be they Barking, Dagenham, East Ham, West Ham, Forest Gate, Plaistow or North Woolwich.

Romford sub-division covered a large rural area, consisting of Romford - the headquarters - Collier Row, Hornchurch, Upminster, Rainham and, to the north, Harold Hill, all former Essex Constabulary police stations. Harold Hill built as a vast council estate for working-class residents, many of whom had moved there from the East End.

An Inspector Morgan who transferred from Essex when the Met took over in 1965 lived in one of the police houses next door to Harold Hill Police Station, and would frequently be found on duty and in full uniform doing his gardening.

On the subject of gardening, during one of my visits to Rainham Police Station, formerly a private residence whose interior rooms were small and staircases narrow, I was met by a couple of the PCs on duty who told me that a young female was in the charge room.

'Who is she?' I enquired.

'Sue. She's a medical student at St Thomas Hospital in London, but lives locally.'

'What's she in for?' I enquired.

The PCs looked rather sheepish but went on to explain.

'She's been arrested for growing cannabis plants.'

'Where?'

'In the window boxes outside.' There was a pause. 'Under our noses!'

I couldn't help but smile when I asked the accused why she had been so brazen. She said it was all in the interests of medical research, although as far as breaking the law was concerned, it had taken some time for anyone to notice.

Before leaving the station to go out on patrol officers usually went to the canteen for a drink of some sort. There was never much choice, but since I never quite got used to the instant coffee lightened with a dash of cold milk, tea was the better option.

Then, either alone or with a colleague, I would start on any non-urgent enquiries or patrol the town centre. As a rookie cop I could hardly resist glancing proudly at my reflection in the shop windows as I walked by. Once I was dressed in my blue serge attire I was ready for action, but we had no stab vests, handcuffs or CS tear spray to use as protection, not even a personal radio, when I was first sent to Division. Back in the Sixties a WPC could walk or drive around their division alone day or night and not feel threatened. In the main we had to rely on the public's respect for authority.

On returning to the nick women officers would report to Sergeant Cross, if she was on duty, about where they had been and what enquiries they had carried out. Apart from checking up on her staff, her role was to assist young WPCs on how to compile certain reports and how to investigate female related enquiries.

'Crossy', as she became known, was a spinster aged around forty. She was a little taller and more buxom than I was. She had tightly permed short blonde hair and a perpetual 'Elizabeth Arden' complexion. Arden had been an advocate for women's rights and once marched past her Red Door Salon on Fifth Avenue alongside 15,000 fellow suffragettes, all wearing red lipstick as a symbol of strength. Red lipstick wouldn't have been Crossy's colour of choice. She had a demure demeanour, but rumour had it that she was having a relationship with one of the married station sergeants. So when in his presence her powdery cheeks tinged a deeper pink, their liaison became apparent.

Working a pattern of day shifts was in itself a strange phenomenon, but I never had to do anything such as night duty before. It all sounded extremely exciting, even though I knew little about what nights might entail.

More often than not nights turned out to be a busy time for WPCs, as any of us could be called to any of the police stations on K Division.

And then if no WPC was available on the neighbouring J Division, we could even be called to one of the stations there, such as Ilford or Barkingside to assist with a female prisoner, child or young person.

During one of my seven nights of duty I was so busy that at one time or other during the week I was needed at every police station on K Division except North Woolwich, a police station north of the division situated close beside the River Thames.

In order to get to the stations where I was required either a police driver would come to collect me, or I would drive there alone through the night from Romford in the GP car.

Romford was always a busy station, but especially so on a Friday or Saturday night. It was and still is a magnet for groups of young people who arrive by train, either having travelled from outer Essex or inner London destinations with the sole intention of having a night out in the town. There were a good many public houses and a few nightclubs where revellers would gather to drink and dance the night away, only to be discharged into the street after last orders or stagger from a nightclub in the early hours of the morning. Many were then ready for a fight with rival factions, sometimes just fuelled by alcohol or through football rivalry, or sometimes just someone taking a dislike to someone else. There was no racial tension in those days, as Havering had the lowest immigrant population. As far as drunkenness was concerned, it makes no distinction between the sexes, but it was often the young women who became the most inebriated. So hardly a late turn or night duty would pass when a WPC would not be needed to assist with drink, and usually disorderly, offences.

It was of course always preferable on night duty to patrol with a PC. But while parked up in a dark alley or similar place in the middle of the night, when nothing could be heard other than the exchange of calls on the car's police radio, some PCs were known to make a pass at their female colleague, often with the excuse that their marriage was on the rocks or their wives continuously accused them of being unfaithful so they might as well be so. There were a couple of incidents where it happened to me, but I was not prepared to be referred to as the station mattress so particularly spurned the advances of married PCs, whose wives didn't understand them!

By 6.00am after a tour of night duty everyone was more than ready to go home for a much-deserved sleep. On one occasion, however, instead of being able to go back to the Upminster hostel I was required to attend Magistrates' Court to give evidence. So I decided I would stay at the Station until 10.00am to catch up on some correspondence and then go next door to the Court. The case was a lengthy one, because the man I had arrested a few weeks earlier for looking up women's skirts as they ascended an escalator in a local store pleaded Not Guilty. So when I eventually got to bed it was about three o'clock in the afternoon. Consequently, when I awoke from a deep slumber I saw it was 10.00pm, and I had overslept for that night's duty! The station sergeant was none too happy with me when I phoned to tell him.

'LATE, for night duty? Get yourself here as soon as possible!'

The allocated shift patterns became a way a life and

body clocks usually adapted quite well, but all officers tended to struggle when it was 'quick changeover' - coming off nights at six o'clock in the morning, getting a few hours sleep and then having to be back at work that afternoon to parade for duty.

Women did not have set beats like male officers so we could patrol any part of the sub-division. Mainly we preferred to go out on foot in the town centre, where most of the action was likely to occur. Under the Metropolitan Police Act 1839, police had the power to stop and search any person who was reasonably suspected of having or conveying in any manner anything stolen or unlawfully obtained, and it was a very useful resource resulting in many successful arrests. But stop and search procedures have been adapted over the years to suit our changing society and cannot be applied as liberally.

While on late turn patrol we could come upon arrestable drinking offences. Most often drunks were good-natured, but in the event of someone being seriously drunk and disorderly, radioing for backup was the sensible option. On the rare occasion of police having to deal with someone who was drunk in charge of a child apparently under the age of seven years, women police would definitely be involved. And those potentially volatile situations such as domestic disputes could often be diffused with what we called 'tact and discretion', avoiding confrontation at all costs. Women police were, and no doubt still are, particularly good at calming such situations.

When on patrol in the market during daylight hours, police would stop to chat with stallholders, many of whom were known criminals or who were connected to notorious Essex families. With a relaxed, polite and friendly approach, police might gather snippets of interesting information about illegal goings on in the Borough such as who was upsetting who, who was wheeling and dealing, sometimes someone even grassed up a relative.

In the market on one such occasion a middle-aged woman beckoned me over to the side of her fruit and veg stall and spoke to me in a hushed tone:

'Officer, my son-in-law is one of the Tobias family, you know that lot?'

'I have heard of them.'

'Well he and his brother is planning a robbery. They're planning to do an offie.'

I considered tact and discretion were definitely necessary in this situation.

'Why are you telling me this?'

'Well, I hate him. I told my daughter he was no good from the day she met him, and then she only goes and marries 'im.'

'Well, Madam, can you give me your name and address so that one of the CID officers can talk to you?'

'You can give them me phone number, wouldn't want them coming round my house.'

'Very well.'

The informant provided me with further details and as soon as I got back to the station I went to see one of the DCs in the CID office.

'Great job, girl, the Tobiases eh. Not surprised they are planning another job. We'll go round the mother-in-law's anyway to see what else she can tell us.'

The following weekend the CID had all the information they needed and an ambush was arranged to ensnare the Junction Road off-licence thieves.

At a pre-arranged time myself and a colleague, in plain clothes, were to park in an unmarked police car as near as practicable to the off-licence. From there we were to observe and record details of the robbery suspects and their getaway car. As closing time for the premises drew near, several police were in place.

It was a particularly dark night, and meagre street lighting and little moonlight did not help our cause, but tensions grew when two Balaclava-clad men appeared and were seen to run into the shop.

A piercing crack of gunfire alerted all the undercover officers, who moved in quickly to make the necessary arrests. Meanwhile, I saw two shadowy figures hastily leave the off-licence and drive off in an awaiting vehicle. Excitedly I shouted to my partner.

'Quick, I've just seen the get-away car, write down this registration number. I'll circulate it to 'All Cars' on the radio.'

An immediate response bounced back from the control room:

'Kilo 4, Kilo 4 you have just circulated the registration number of the CID car! OVER!'

Red faced, I returned to the station.

I had not on this occasion been much use to the team. But I was pleased to know the Tobiases had been stopped by the CID as they were attempting to drive away in their car, and were duly arrested for theft and firearm offences. Fortunately, no harm had come to the manager of the off-licence but for me the incident was a steep learning curve and I would never make such an embarrassing mistake again.

If at any time I was attached as 'Aid' to the CID, as I was for the 'offie' job, a plain clothes allowance was claimable, although on that occasion I hardly deserved any. There was also an additional payment known as 'Refs', which could be claimed for refreshments if one was required to work beyond a normal shift. All officers worked their ARD – an additional rest day – for which we got paid. But we could take off any overtime that was accrued, usually saved up until a few hours or days could be taken at one time. Officers often volunteered to do crowd control duty at matches at West Ham's stadium for paid overtime.

One Night Duty I was called to deal with a female prisoner at West Ham Police Station, and while there one of the older PCs noticed my divisional number.

'80K,' he mused.

'Yes, so?'

'We had a Sergeant 80K here once.'

The old boys, PCs with long service, always had a tale to tell, but this connection intrigued me more than usual.

'Go on.'

'In 1961 a crazed 30-year-old fugitive pilot came into this nick to hand himself in after seriously assaulting his wife, his mother and his step-sister. When asked by the interviewing officer, Detective Inspector George Jones, to empty his pockets, the pilot produced a pistol and began shooting. Then the gunman ran out.'

'Where does 80K come into this?'

'Well,' the PC continued. 'Police Sergeant 80K Frederick Hutchins and a colleague took a car and went in pursuit of the gunman. They spotted him in Tennyson Road. Sergeant Hutchins tackled the gunman to the ground, but when he got to his feet he shot the two officers, and Hutchins died.'

'How dreadful.' I sighed.

'Moments later Inspector Philip Pawsey, who was driving to work received a radio message about an armed man, but he was also shot dead. Then the gunman shot at another officer, Police Constable Leslie England, who was on a motorbike, but he managed to swerve the bullets and the gunman made off down Romford Road where police lost sight of him.'

At that point I was called away to see the woman prisoner who had been arrested for assault earlier that evening during a pub brawl. I had to search her for possible possession of drugs or objects with which she could self-harm. Then take her fingerprints by rolling her fingers and thumbs over an ink-covered slide and then press each one onto a fingerprint form that was then sent off to Fingerprint Branch at the Yard for analysis. Fingerprinting has come a long way since those messy ink days.

Before I left West Ham station I found the PC in the canteen who had been telling me the story about the tragedy.

'Charlie, was the gunman ever caught?'

'Sort of,' he continued after a mouthful of tea. 'You see, later that evening, the gunman went to a phone box at Wanstead Flats and called the *Sunday Express* news desk. The reporter who answered managed to get him to reveal his location. Then the newspaper informed police, which led to officers surrounding the phone box before the gunman shot himself. He died in hospital of his injuries.'

'How was Sergeant Hutchins remembered?'

'He received the posthumous QPM for bravery. But his divisional number has never been given out to anyone else 'til now.'

I never questioned why 80K was allocated to me, but

A Girl in Blue

the story I was told that day at West Ham Police Station sent a chill down my spine, especially hearing how an officer could suddenly be struck down in the line of duty, making the ultimate sacrifice.

As I got more and more familiar with my work, I was aware that my male colleagues not only surveyed my petite figure, but tested my aptitude for dealing with difficult incidents. It was therefore no surprise when the Station Sergeant assigned me to a particularly sensitive enquiry.

'Lass, there is a stiff in Oldchurch Hospital mortuary for you to check out.'

The form of address seemed over-familiar, the precursor of sexual harrassment may I add, but there was a job to do so I accepted the order.

Unbeknown to me, the mortician had been forewarned by the station officer that a rookie cop was being sent to look at one of the bodies.

'Who have you come to see?' he asked.

I gave him the name of the deceased: 'Margaret Smith.'

Then he slid open one of the steel drawers to expose a corpse with a name tag tied to its toe.

'It's not this one.' He paused. 'I'll try the next.'

'Margaret. A female?' I repeated the details.

'Oh sorry that was a man. Next!'

The mortician continued to reveal especially selected exhibits until he came upon the one I needed to look at. Eventually I was shown the intended deceased and left with a wry smile on my face as I bade him a cheery 'Good day'.

Back at the nick no-one had the nerve to ask me how I had got on, and I considered the initiation to be a far better one than the infamous 'station stamp', which fortunately none of my male colleagues ever had the chance to print on my bottom!

Then, one Saturday as I arrived for early turn, Crossy called me into her office.

'Lately we have received several reports from members of the public saying that their purses have been stolen.'

I could feel an order heading my way.

'As you are the only WPC on duty this morning I want you to go to the Market Place to see what's what.'

'Yes Sarge.'

'Oh, and by the way as you are still a Probationer, I am sending PC Russell to do the obs with you.'

A short walk from the police station and the nearby Civic Hall stands the historical Romford market, first established by Royal Charter in 1247 for selling livestock. By 1967 animals were no longer sold, but the street market had become one of the largest in the south east with over one hundred and fifty stalls offering a diverse range of goods including fresh meat and fish, vegetables and fruit, the latest fashions and household goods.

PC Russell, known as Rusty, was a much-liked officer who had the swagger of an East End spiv with an accent to match. He, like me, was already in civvies, and together we left the nick by the back door.

'Have you ever arrested a pickpocket?' I asked him.

'Cor Luv, I've nicked more than you've had hot dinners. Don't worry if it happens, just do what you have to do.'

The Theft Act and Judges Rules were mulled over in my head as we walked down Main Road towards the market.

'Now, mingle with the shoppers, and if you are jostled in the crowd expect your purse to be gone.'

'OK.'

Rusty continued with his advice.

'I'll keep you in my sights, but just make sure the loot is not handed over to a third player, an accomplice, 'cos if that 'appens you're snookered.'

The stooge purse lay half-hidden in the shopping basket of previously prepared fruit and veg, typical market purchases.

'Mind your purse love.' An elderly lady warned me to cover it up.

I thanked her and moved away, only to reveal it again as planned.

The market was already bustling with shoppers, and the stallholders' cries promoting their wares floated overhead.

After about half an hour, a middle-aged man brushed past me taking the purse with him, and as he did so I saw him swiftly deposit it into his jacket pocket. Instinctively, I grabbed him by the arm and produced my warrant card, telling him I was a police officer. For a second the man looked at me in disbelief, but then pulled away and turned straight into the arms of Rusty.

'The lady wants to have a word with you mate.'

'You have stolen my purse; you are not obliged to say anything unless you wish to do so, but what you say may be put into writing and given as evidence.'

There was no reply.

Rusty had the man's arm up behind his back, and in seconds had found a number of purses secreted within the accused's various pockets. Rusty knew exactly which pocket my stolen purse was in, having kept me thoroughly in his sights.

'I am arresting you for theft of my purse.' I informed the man, and continued with the obligatory caution.

'Piss off cunt,' was his reply.

Although practical experience on the streets was an essential part of the job, initially I was unprepared for the names I or my colleagues were likely to be called.

'Old Bill' was one of the most familiar names by which police were referred, although no-one seems certain of its origin.

In the 1860s there was a Sergeant Bill Smith at Limehouse Police Station. He was a popular character and people used to ask after 'Old Bill'. Another possible origin was because in the past many police officers wore authoritarian-style moustaches, like adorning a famous WWI cartoon character 'the wily old soldier in the trenches' by Bruce Bairnsfather. In 1917 the Government used Bairnsfather's character in posters and advertisements, putting across war-time messages under the banner 'Old Bill says…' In this campaign the character was dressed in a Special Constable's uniform. Lastly, I heard that the Flying Squad, created in 1919, was the first to use cars, so that they could pursue criminals into any Met division. All of their vehicles had the registration letters BYL, consequently the Squad became known as the 'The Bill'.

So along with Old Bill and any other derogatory remarks such as filth, scum and pig, I soon found it necessary to turn a deaf ear.

'Name,' I demanded.

'Dickie Bird.'

'Address?'

Somehow I sensed what his next response might be.

'Upper Tree.'

His making things difficult didn't make much difference as he was arrested, so Rusty and I took the man to the

A Girl in Blue

market office where the three of us awaited for a patrol car to convey us to the police station rather than frog march the prisoner through the streets.

Rusty whispered, 'You alright love?'

'Fine,' I replied as I shakily wrote down the details of my first arrest in my pocketbook.

In the charge room the accused and I were met by the Station Sergeant.

'What you got girl?'

I related the facts concerning 'what I'd got' and the station officer was satisfied with my evidence, so the accused was formerly charged with the offence of theft.

He appeared at Romford Magistrates' Court the next day, where thankfully he pleaded guilty so I was saved from giving evidence. As expected details of the man's previous theft-related convictions were read out, together with his antecedent history. The Magistrate awarded a term of imprisonment and 'Dickie Bird' was retained at Her Majesty's Pleasure for the mandatory time.

With that arrest over, I was eager to carry on doing what I had been trained to do, and training itself did not stop. The first two years of employment as a police officer was known as the Probation period, during which monthly District Training at the divisional HQ, in my case Romford, had to be attended. I joined a small class of male probationers to be instructed by an Inspector about new and current legislation, as well as undergoing regular testing on various aspects of the law. Failure to reach the required standard at the end of the two years would mean dismissal.

On one occasion when I was the only WPC on duty on the sub-division, I was sent to make enquiries about a young person who had been reported missing from a house in Dagenham, a predominately residential council estate mostly built to house employees of nearby Ford Motors in 1931. The address I had been given was beyond walking distance from Romford, so I obtained a lift from a patrolling officer who was able to drop me at the location before heading off to an enquiry of his own.

When I had finished my enquiry I realised I had been abandoned in Dagenham's interior, a vast maze of identical-looking houses. So I walked along a few neighbouring streets until I came upon a Police Box, a telephone kiosk located in a public place for the use of police officers or members of the public to contact the police.[5]

I opened the hatch with the key attached to my whistle chain to access the black Bakelite telephone and I lifted the receiver.

'Scotland Yard here,' a stern voice bellowed from within.

'Hello, this is WPC 80K, attached to Romford Police

---

5 A thousand such boxes existed in London at one time, but there were none on Havering's ground due to it being formerly Essex Constabulary so it was a novelty find for me. Such boxes were installed in 1929, the first in Richmond and Wood Green. They were constructed of pre-cast reinforced concrete about nine feet high, placed on a wide base. The box had a shallow pyramid-shaped roof which rose in three tiered steps, with a light fixed to the apex which was housed within a protective mesh with a domed top. Each side bore a sign saying 'POLICE'. A metal-framed window housed six panes of glass, the upper row being clear and the bottom row containing frosted glass. The central pane was blue-tinted, so a blue light was visible externally when the box was lit from the inside. The front of the kiosk had a teak door on the right-hand side and a fixed panel on the left. The upper part had a square hatch, which when opened provided a telephone to call the emergency services. The bottom part held a First Aid kit behind a door, which could only be opened with a key obtained by breaking a small glass panel. The interior housed a high bench and a stool to match, room enough for just one person.

Station.'

'How can I assist?'

'Well, I am lost somewhere in the middle of Dagenham.'

'This phone is only supposed to be used in an emergency!'

'I consider my being lost without any way of getting back to base an emergency!'

Begrudgingly the information room operator said, 'Stay where you are and I'll send a car to fetch you.'

So that was my one and only experience of a Police Box but a couple of years later, the powers that were, possibly the London County Council, decided to start decommissioning the boxes with the majority being removed or demolished in-situ. The last box in London was removed by 1981, but its reputation lives on in the form of the TARDIS in the BBC's *Doctor Who*.

On another occasion, as soon as I had booked on for early turn duty a CID officer put his head round my office door and shouted, 'We need you!' There was no further explanation but from the look on his face I wasn't going to argue, so I put on my hat and threw my gabardine mac over my uniform, checked I had my pocket book and hurried after him. The CID officer - Henry - and I met our uniform police driver in the yard and the three of us got into an unmarked vehicle, a blue Hillman Hunter.

On the way to our destination, Henry explained further.

'We've had a call from the staff at Gidea Park railway station to say that a baby has been found abandoned in the waiting room.' It had been raining steadily since dawn so there was some consolation that the child was inside; although we had no idea what condition the poor thing might be in.

It took less than five minutes to get to our destination,

weaving precariously through the rush hour traffic. When we arrived we jumped out of the car and one-by-one slammed the doors of the vehicle behind us. That experience alone was quite exhilarating for me, as it was how I had seen actors in *Z Cars* and *Dixon of Dock Green* abuse their cars, but this was reality. We ran into the railway station and saw that an ambulance had arrived there before us, and the two-man crew were attending to the newborn baby boy. One of the ambulance crew dispelled our fears as he called out to us:

'He's alive and we've wrapped him up warmly against the cold.'

'Was there a note, or anything attached to identify him?' I asked.

'No, he's just got on a blue Babygro.'

'Where are you taking him?'

'Oldchurch.' Romford's main hospital was a twenty minute drive from where we were.

Thereafter, our job was to work with the CID to gather any information about the circumstances of the abandonment in an attempt to trace the child's mother.

As the CID officers grew to trust my capabilities, I would be called upon to assist if and when a female officer in plain clothes was needed. And there were a few occasions when, unable to extract a confession from a male suspect, a CID officer would use me as the 'good cop' with the gentle touch in order to question and extract what was needed.

'Now the CID officer has asked you if you received stolen goods from a known offender.'

'Yeah.'

'You have denied any involvement.'

No answer.

Then I began to ask the suspect about his home life and family circumstances. This approach generally encouraged the suspect to open up and admit the error of his ways, and allow me to take the necessary admission statement. Such measures were far from easy but always worth a try, and took place long before the days of the codes of practice introduced by the Police and Criminal Evidence Act of 1984 which set out to strike the right balance between the powers of the police and the rights and freedoms of the public.

A few months after arriving in Romford, I witnessed a CID officer holding a suspect by his ankles as he dangled him out of the first floor office window in an attempt to extract a confession. Another time I witnessed a police colleague push a suspect into the police station broom cupboard, again to extract a confession.

One could argue that there was no excuse for such conduct, but in both cases these hardened criminals were found to be guilty and although the police are not judge nor jury, in the interests of public safety such characters need to be denied their freedom for a few years at least.

Lois aged 2-years-old
outside the Royston Hotel

Aged three, with her father
Bill Clark

Family outing: Lois (front) with her mother,
stepsister Brenda and stepbrother Ralph

Lois's stepfather Douglas Brignall,
dressed in his Ordnance Corps uniform

The class of Metropolitan Police recruits of March 1967 in the quadrant at the rear of the Peel House building, known as Savile Row. Of the five women in the centre, Lois is second from the right (first WPC on the right-hand page). The senior officers and instructors are in the front row; Tommy Wall, the infamous Superintendent of the Training School, is front row centre (far-right on left page)

Class of '67 dressed for a Crown Court visit. L-R: Lois, Carol Hood, ?, Linda Bailey, Muriel Lea

Lois (right) listens intently as Sgt Cross gives details of an assignment, 1967

Lois at Romford Police Station, 1968

Women officers attached to Romford Police Station, 1968.
L-R: Pat Howe, Pat Atkins, Sgt Edith Cross, Daphne Acton, WPC 80K Willoughby

Upminster Police Station. The WPC Hostel was at the right hand side

Upminster Hostel message book entry

1969: a group of Women Police at the rear of Barking Police Station wearing the uniform designed by Norman Hartnell. Those in civvies were the then 'Juvenile Bureau' officers. Lois second right.

West End Central Vice Squadm 1971.
PC John Summers (Lois's brother-in-law) is fourth from the left

Lois's 21st Birthday party, 1969

Lois in the Women Police Office at Romford Station, 1970

A group of Women Police outside Romford Police Station in 1970, having a farewell gathering for Pat H, seen with her parents and sisters before leaving for Australia to become a Police officer there. Sgt Cross, in civvies, and Lois are kneeling, left side

1967
The Summer of Love

In 1965, the Dangerous Drugs Act was passed and implemented the 'Brain Committee' recommendations of giving police powers to stop and search suspected handlers of cannabis.

Had I been a police officer in 1965 I could have directed them to a certain club in Forest Hill where plenty of dope and purple tablets were available. However, two years after the Dangerous Drugs Act was passed a campaign was started to legalise 'pot', stating 'The law against marijuana is immoral in principle and unworkable in practice.'

Signatories who supported the campaign included The Beatles, RD Laing and Graham Greene. But the 1965 Act remained.

The summer of 1967 went on to become known as 'The Summer of Love', and it was celebrated throughout the land. The younger generation all wanted to go to San Francisco to wear flowers in their hair, but for the local youth, Romford had to do. A crowd of hippies, otherwise known as 'Flower Children', decided to gather on Sunday, 8th August in Romford's Raphael Park for a 'love in', believing that flowers, the symbol of love, would conquer all.

A Girl in Blue

Due to the expectation of a large gathering of youths and onlookers, the local paper had run a story advertising the event, police, myself included, were sent to the park to keep order and be prepared for any misconduct. We were all in uniform, although there were some officers deployed in plain clothes dressed as mods infiltrating the event. The police summer uniform was referred to as 'shirt sleeve order'; no tunic jackets had to be worn, but our long shirt sleeves - white for women, blue for the men - were rolled up above our elbows. Short sleeve shirts had not yet been designed for us.

The event itself was organised by a local hippie named Cornelius, who with his long hair and afghan coat had mustered up some like-minded people to assemble and embrace the symbolism. Boys dressed in flower-patterned shirts, with more flowers painted on their cheeks, walked hand-in-hand with girls wearing micro-mini skirts and rows of long beads or small bells round their necks and the obligatory flowers in their hair. Many were spaced-out, reading poetry or embroiled with topics ranging from apartheid to the Nuclear Bomb. Others were seemingly content just blowing up condoms and patting them around.

As it turned out there were more police than hippies in Raphael Park that afternoon, and our superior officers told us only to move in if trouble did erupt. I stood in an elevated position on the park bandstand beside some shade-giving trees enjoying the atmosphere and surveying the scene, but suddenly there were shouts!

'We are being invaded!'

We could all see a large crowd of trouble-making youths coming into the park with the sole purpose of breaking up the event and to silence the groups of hippy

The Summer of Love

minstrels and buskers who were playing music by the likes of Joan Baez, Dylan and Donovan.

The invaders started chanting 'West Ham! West Ham!', drowning out the protest songs. Football thugs surely had something better to do on a sunny afternoon, but obviously not on this occasion. They joined hands and danced around one of the police patrol cars positioned by the park gates. On seeing trouble brewing my colleagues and I ran to rescue the two PCs who were trapped in their car, but on the arrival of police the unruly gang dispersed and fled along Main Road.

As well as that short-lived affray, police also had to deal with the traffic congestion in Main Road created by bemused sightseers, and during the afternoon a few revellers were arrested for possession of drugs, mainly pot.

That same summer, information was received by Romford Police about a particular group of teenage hippies who were planning to gather in Upminster Woods for a 'Pot Party'. During a briefing at Upminster Police Station, a short distance from the targeted venue, several uniformed officers were ordered to remain at the entrance of the woods, then myself and a sergeant, both in plain clothes, were sent in to investigate.

It was about ten o'clock at night when we arrived at the woods. Darkness had fallen, and the further we moved into them the darker it got. We crept stealthily, all the time trying to avoid the twigs that crunched noisily beneath our feet. We had our torches but could not use them for fear of attracting attention, so it took us about an hour until we could see the glow of a campfire and heard the low chanting of Peter, Paul and Mary's *Blowing in the Wind*. Satisfied that drug-related offences were taking place - we could smell the weed as we approached - we blew our whistles and made our surprise entrance.

'Nobody move. We are police officers!'

The six young people, mostly in their late teens, tried to scatter but their attempt was thwarted as they were faced with the back-up that had been on standby around the woods. In turn several arrests were made for possession of cannabis.

1967-68

Comrades

After a while, Carol and I rarely saw one another because when she was on leave she would most often go and stay with her fiancé in north London.

But my own new-found independence was liberating, especially where shopping and cooking was concerned. Together with the transistor radio, my mother had also given me a recipe book. She collected cookery books like some people collect novels, so I was able to create a variety of basic fayre and not starve like my mother had thought I might.

A real luxury for all of us was that we had a cleaner, as a lady from the town was employed by the police to visit the hostel once a week. She was not exactly thorough, but her contribution saved us much time and energy. There was also a small garden at the back of the premises, but none of us had any inclination to tend it so it was not much more than scrubby grass, somewhere to sit out on hot days, but mainly it remained a space for hanging out our washing.

In the narrow passage leading from the front door to the stairs was a wall telephone. This connected the residents of the hostel to the police station switchboard next door. Understandably, the officers on duty were inclined to get annoyed if we made or received too many personal phone calls. But since the telephone reception was often poor and crackly, and there was also the chance the operator on the other side of the wall might be listening in, we soon realised it was better to use the phone only as a necessity. But if the dreaded phone happened to ring at 6.00am or earlier, we inmates knew it would be a call for the Early Turn WPC to go into work earlier to relieve the night duty WPC; a female officer who would have been involved with a woman prisoner or young person during the night, either of whom was still in custody or detained. In such cases, the sergeant at the station concerned would send a PC in the GP car or van to pick up whichever one of us was needed.

After a few months, Beryl resigned, left the hostel and went back to Derbyshire to marry a farmer; Rita resigned and was replaced by Daphne, who had worked at New Scotland Yard before joining the police. Towards the end of 1967, Daphne arrived wearing the newly-introduced, Norman Hartnell-designed women police uniform. I intended to hang on to my 'Bather' uniform for as long as possible, but in 1968 I was forced to exchange it for the more modern design; a shapeless double-breasted blue serge jacket, an A-line skirt, white shirt with an attached collar and a flat black bow tie fixed to the shirt with a strip of velcro.

The soft dark blue hat with a shiny black peak may have suited a female flight attendant on an aeroplane, but offered little or no protection to one's head in an affray, unlike the sturdy helmets supplied to PCs. Our only cold-weather outer garment was a dark woollen cape, secured at the neck with a chain link, but if one had to give chase while wearing it the public would surely have likened the sight to Batman, or more likely Robin, his junior counterpart.

Finally, instead of the tunic breast pockets of the Bather design, we were provided with a black leather shoulder bag in which to keep necessary 'appointments', pocketbooks and a truncheon. Fortunately, with the coming of the Hartnell design we did not have to relinquish our whistle and chain. But due to its unpopularity, emphasizing style over practicality, the Hartnell uniform lasted only until 1972 when it was replaced by the 'Surrey' design, which I never got to wear.

The Women Police uniform has from the beginning always undergone change, but an amusing extract from an historic Police Order once stated: 'The navy blue knickers issued to women police will be withdrawn and replaced with collars and ties!' An interesting notion.

Daphne had undergone the usual interview process at Borough High Street, but at 5' 3" she was found to be one inch below the acceptable height. However, the panel happened to be in possession of a letter she had written to New Scotland Yard when she was thirteen, asking if she could be allowed to join the Police Cadets when she was sixteen. At that time girls were not accepted into the Cadets, so in the meantime Daphne decided to take an office job at New Scotland Yard and continued to develop her fitness and in time became a blue belt at judo. Seeing how determined she was to be a police constable, the Met received special dispensation from the Home Office to overlook her one inch height limitation and in due course she was accepted.

After the struggle she underwent to gain entry, Daphne was also somewhat disappointed to be posted to the edge of the metropolis but soon became an effective officer.

Daphne and I were only six months apart in age and

similarly built, scarcely passing the five foot four height requirement. I became her mentor for a few weeks until she had familiarised herself with the layout of Romford's ground and the various communities.

Overall, she dealt with everything that came her way. She was delighted when she arrested an illegal trader in Romford market and then escorted him to the Station. On arrival in the charge room the detainee declared, 'I've never been so humiliated in my life, being nabbed and walked through the town by a female copper. Perhaps worse than the amount I'm likely to be fined.'

But after one tour of duty in particular I found her in the lounge of the Upminster hostel. She looked more forlorn than I had ever seen her before.

'What's up Daph?' I enquired.

'Bit of a rough day.'

'Why?'

At first she was reluctant to show any sign of emotion, but eventually she took a deep breath.

'I got a call today to go to Dagenham's ground to tell a woman her husband had fallen out of a painting cradle when it tipped over.'

'Was he lost?'

'Yes, it was a horrible thing to tell her. He had been working in the cradle beside a building overhanging a canal or river and he was missing, feared dead.'

I knew it was the first time Daphne had had to deliver a death notice to a relative, but thereafter she found such incidents easier to handle. She had to remain particularly stoic when she was the first officer to go to see parents of two young girls who had been reported missing but were later found dead, an infamous case known as the Babes in the Wood murders.

No officer is that cold-hearted not to be affected by such sad incidents, never completely erasing them from memory. But it was and is all in the line of duty and life goes on.

After Daphne was settled in, the two Pats arrived from Training School. In order to differentiate them, one was known as Tish and the other Pat H. The latter was a couple of years older than the rest of us. She had a strong accent, wavy auburn hair and could not be mistaken for anything other than Irish. We discovered she was the eldest of a large number of siblings, whereas Tish, fair-haired with a slim boyish figure, was the only child of elderly parents, and hailed from Aberdeen.

As previously mentioned, the paths of women officers at Romford at that time rarely crossed, either in the hostel or at the station. Therefore it was decided to create a message book that became an invaluable method for passing on information about work or housekeeping.

A typical entry in the hostel message book would read:

> Dear All, Re: Romford Missing Person enquiry.
>
> FYI - A woman has gone missing from her home address. She has been gone for 48 hours. She has not taken any belongings and only has £16 in her possession. She is on regular medication for depression. The informant is her husband who is staying at his grandmother's address for the time being.

Whoever was next on duty at Romford would digest this information and be expected to make decisions about the investigation.

Much of the work of women police centred on trying to find people reported missing; an intriguing part of our work, like a jigsaw puzzle waiting to be solved.

A Girl in Blue

These enquiries were usually solved quickly, but could sometimes take weeks to solve depending on the circumstances.

Missing children or Approved School absconders took priority and would always be investigated thoroughly, whereas adults would only be so if they went missing under unusual circumstances. A case we did not pursue but did hear about later concerned a man who walked out on his family and disappeared, but months later ended up in Australia. Another man who was diagnosed with terminal cancer ended his life by jumping in front of a train at Elm Park station.

In order to discover the motives or circumstances under which someone went missing, the home address would be visited and relatives and friends interviewed. The information gathered would be collated and police would visit locations the missing person was known to frequent. On the odd occasion, parents refused to be repatriated with their wayward offspring so the child or young person would have to be taken by police to Juvenile Court, a special Court for people aged between the ages of ten and seventeen (ten being the age of criminal responsibility) as being in need of Care and Protection, although this was something we tried to avoid for fear of escalating the problem. More often than not enquiries into a missing person had satisfactory conclusions, but every case was different.

> Local Dagenham girl found, was at Oldchurch Hospital – lost memory.
>
> To whom it may concern...
>
> Can you start work earlier at 1.00pm as there are two approved school absconders in at Romford, and the WPC on duty needs some assistance.

Comrades

Anita, an Approved School absconder, is in custody overnight on H Division – Leman Street nick. The Approved School will collect her at Dagenham at 11am on Sunday. However, you will probably have to escort her. Have left a note for Sergeant Cross. So you are forearmed. The girl is a runner but she is OK if you chat to her etc.

Another memorable entry was written in the hostel information book by the night duty WPC when she arrived home in the early hours:

Whoever is on Early Turn duty at KD (7.12.69). - Special attention requested.
Overnight - Temporary DC's wife reported missing.

It was my turn on Earlies that day, and when I arrived the station sergeant called me into the front office.

'Morning, glad it's you I have a missing person enquiry.'

'Is it Ray Vaughn's wife?' I anticipated the answer, for Ray had had cause to report her missing on a previous occasion but I had not been involved in the enquiry that time.

'Yes, Yvonne. She was reported missing last night and under the circumstances, we are taking this very seriously.'

'What has been done so far Sarge?'

'The make and model of her car was circulated last night as soon as she was reported missing. Naturally everything possible has been covered. It's a colleague's missus and everyone is very worried. Time is of the essence.'

Ray was a tall, handsome man with golden brown hair and a complexion to match. He was a known philanderer and it was no secret that his wife had previously made several attempts on her life.

'Have police contacted all her known friends and relatives to ask if she has been seen?'

'Yes, no trace.'

I knew that Ray and Yvonne had three children.

'Where are the kids?' I asked.

'They're ok. They're with their Gran.'

'And where is Ray?'

'He is upstairs and I want you to take a statement from him.'

Taking statements was bread and butter work for a Women Police Officer, but interviewing a colleague was going to need a greater deal of empathy.

I found him slumped at his desk in the CID office, anguish and sleep deprivation marring his usual charming persona.

I sat down in the chair next to him and was the first to speak.

'Ray, I'm afraid,' I heard myself saying the very words that should never leave a police officer's lips, so restarted.

'Ray, I'm sorry I have been asked to take a statement from you about the events leading up to your wife's disappearance.'

'Go ahead.'

'When did you last see Yvonne?'

'Last night at dinner.'

'At home?'

'Yes.'

'Did you notice anything unusual about her behaviour?'

'Not at dinner, but after.'

'Why was that?'

'I told her I was going out.'

'What time was that?'
'Seven thirty.'
'Did you go out?'
'No.'

I began Ray's statement with the mandatory - day, date, time and place - and questioned him about the events of the previous evening.

'Why didn't you go out?'
'We had a terrible row and she walked out.'
'What did you argue about?'

Through gossip and supposition I had a fair idea what the reason was, and Ray was prepared to tell me. He had developed more than a working relationship with Stella, who in fact was one of my colleagues. She had transferred from the Essex Constabulary to the Met in 1965, as Ray had also chosen to do, and they ended up working at the same station, she in uniform and he attached to the CID.

'Stella.'
'Did you then go out as planned?
'No. I couldn't leave the kids.'
'Did she take her car?'
'Yes.'

Then, just as Ray was about to sign his completed statement, a senior officer entered the room and called him to one side. In a hushed tone Ray was informed that his wife had been found dead in her car with the engine running in a lock-up garage. A handwritten note beside her lifeless body was testament to the fact that she knew about her husband's affair.

Ray Vaughn remained in the Met until his retirement, but very soon after the tragedy Stella left the country and emigrated to South Africa. So this was one of those missing person's enquiries with no happy ending.

Whilst on duty a WPC would more than likely be asked - or in fact expected - to make the drinks for her male colleagues, especially if the canteen in the police station was closed.

In fact I always preferred to manage the after-hours kitchen myself during Night Duty or Late Turn in Romford Police Station, where there was a sink, a fridge and an electric kettle on the same floor as the regular canteen, rather than having one of the men let loose there. (Do men wash their hands after going to the toilet like they profess?)

The general cry of the shift during a refreshment break would be 'Come on Plonk, tea all round!'

'A Plonk' was what women police officers were called to differentiate the girls from the boys. The term, some might now consider derogatory, but as well was meant to describe a cheap wine or a 'Person of little or no knowledge', its actual origin is not really known and being called such was taken for granted.

Ordinarily, incidents of intimidation were rare but if they did occur I knew how to give as good as I got; salt instead of sugar in someone's beverage usually did the trick.

The old school ex-Essex coppers, many of whom had been in the armed forces before joining the police, had had little experience of working with women so in the main they were much more chauvinistic than the Met men. Many male officers believed women were an invasion of what should have been a purely masculine preserve.

But it was possible for things to go too far, as illustrated one day when there were several women officers out on patrol and a message was transmitted over everyone's radio.

'Calling all Bras, calling all Bras. WPC needed at KD.'

On another occasion soon after her arrival at Romford my colleague Daphne was at work one night when the men of the night duty shift decided they needed to perform her initiation ceremony.

'WPC Acton!' a PC called out. 'You are wanted in the front office.' There, Daphne was grabbed by two of the younger PCs while about four others looked on. She was laid out flat on her back on the front counter. Her shirt was lifted up and a date-stamp was printed on her stomach. All she could do was to laugh along with them in order to avoid being tarnished as a prude.

Having become aware that such behaviour existed we women officers were prepared to take a joke, but the way a woman officer could respond was either ignore it or, if one was particularly upset, the only course of action was to submit a written report to a senior officer. However, unless a woman could prove that an actual offence had been committed any undesirable behaviour would have been considered all part of the job. It was not until late in the 20th century that appropriate sexual harassment legislation came into force to protect employees.

However, before such legislation existed, revenge could take a variety of forms. One way was to be reluctant to help an offending male colleague with a complex case involving women or children, for PCs knew that WPCs could manage such cases with a high level of efficiency. Or we might be unwilling to assist with any typing they needed doing. For I and many WPCs had been taught to type, either at school or in some former employment.

One might say that there shouldn't have been any

intimidation by the male officers, but one has to remember that little under fifty years prior to my joining the Job, Police Orders for 22nd November 1918 outlined the formation of the women police in London. Mrs Sofia Stanley was appointed the Superintendent, under whom ten supervisors directed one hundred female police officers. Not many at all considering the size of London. Thereafter, progress in recruiting women in any large numbers continued to be slow until well after integration in the Seventies.

All officers, whatever rank, had to rely on one another when dealing with any incident, and the strong sense of camaraderie ensured that women watched out for the men as much as they did for us. I think harassment happened with the arrival of political correctness and some people took advantage of it. Today it appears that officer's comrades, whether male or female, whom we could rely on in the past, are now expected to look out for themselves. But the moderating factor in terms of people's behaviour that helps the police to be at the top of their game is the advent of mobile phone cameras worn on officers' uniforms.

So my life and that of the other WPCs who worked on Romford sub-division and resided in the Upminster hostel continued. Whenever we saw one another, usually at changeover time, we got on well and in the hostel relationships were good, although someone might eat someone's food rations or forget to replenish the milk. But when any of us was on night duty it was the responsibility of the early or late turn WPC to ensure that there were at least the basics in the fridge for when we got home for breakfast or for when we got up around 2 o'clock in the afternoon. There were times when kitchen equipment got broken but in the event, the only course of action was to hide anything of that nature from Crossy until we could get it fixed ourselves.

There was no television installed in the house as it was not considered a necessity by the police accommodation service, but on my arrival I organised the rental of a colour set from Radio Rentals in Upminster. Although at times I had to remind my housemates about their share of the fee.

So communal living in the hostel didn't always run smoothly. Occasionally one of us might invite a boyfriend round for a meal, thus invading someone else's space. Or we would risk having a boyfriend to stay over, especially if they had no transport or the last District Line train had gone. Then one morning, as one such friend was leaving my room, he came face-to-face with Pat H, who was up early preparing to go to work.

'What do you think you are doing here at this time?'

Red-faced he brushed past her and quickly left the premises, but even though she knew him as my regular boyfriend the encounter was sufficient for Pat to decide to report me to Crossy.

Later in the day I was summoned to her office.

'It has come to my attention that you allowed a man to stay in your room overnight. Last night in fact?'

'Yes Sarge.'

'Well you are aware, no doubt, that I will have to report you to a senior officer?'

I wasn't sure which senior officer was going to deal with my reported misdemeanour, but a day or two later I was summoned to Scotland Yard to face the wrath of the woman Superintendent Win Taylor.

Scotland Yard was a formidable place, built of red brick alongside the River Thames. Inside I found it similar to

A Girl in Blue

the Victorian school I had attended, where your every step bounced off the white tiled walls.

After being summoned into Miss Taylor's office I realised there was another senior officer present. Both of them sat behind a large oak desk looking down at an array of papers and correspondence. I hoped none of it appertained to me but Miss Taylor raised her eyes and glared.

'WPC Willoughby, please explain to us the circumstances of how a young man ended up staying in the Upminster hostel with you. I understand he stayed the night in your room?'

'Ma'am,' I had to answer carefully in my defence for the outcome of the construed misdemeanour could have resulted in an end to my career in the force. 'It is what my colleague reported.'

'Well was that the case?'

'I had been out with the said young man, but after dropping me off at the Hostel, his car broke down outside and he was unable to summon the AA until the morning. So I suggested he could stay.'

The car of the boyfriend in question was unreliable at the best of times. On another occasion in the early hours he had left the hostel but on driving away in his sports car the front nearside of the vehicle collapsed when one of the wheels broke off. The noise alerted a couple of officers on night duty in the police station next door, but fortunately they were pleased to have something to do during an otherwise quiet night so somehow managed to fix the offending axle.

'The fact that he stayed in the hostel overnight is a serious contravention of the rules. You know that don't you?'

'Yes Ma'am.'

The two senior officers muttered something to one another while I contemplated a none too satisfactory conclusion.

'Miss Willoughby, as you are of previous good behaviour we are willing to overlook the whole incident.'

I stifled the tears! Get a grip woman, not wanting to show such a pathetic emotion, in full uniform too.

I left HQ and made my way back to Upminster on the train and to the hostel. Never again did I speak to Pat H, although it was not long before she moved out for good.

At one time during my occupancy there was a period of almost a year when I was the only resident. Women police were either leaving the division or getting married, so although it was in one way enjoyable having the place to myself, it was at times a lonely, solitary existence, especially when my twentieth birthday proved to be celebration-free.

As time went on I was reluctant to risk the wrath of my superiors again, but I did allow Graham to stay for a few hours with me in the hostel when we were both off duty whilst being forever mindful of a possible impromptu visit from Sergeant Cross. The rear upstairs bedroom windows overlooked the police station yard where she could be seen to park her car.

'Crossy! Quick get your things.'

Inside the police station she would linger a while to lap up the attention paid to her by any of the PCs on duty there, then she would leave by the front doors of the nick and head next door to the hostel, thus allowing us precious practised time to clear the premises.

1968-69

Policing Romford

One evening in April 1968, a famous pop group was performing live on stage at the Odeon cinema in Romford. I was on duty in uniform at the police station when a distressed mother came in to report her fourteen-year-old daughter missing.

'My baby, my baby, my life already!' She sobbed as she fell to the floor, somewhat gracefully.

I helped the woman to her feet. She was not much more than 40-years-old, with dyed blonde bouffant hair and heavy make-up.

'She's besotted with the band that is playing in Romford tonight.' The woman continued to howl, 'I told her she couldn't go, and she's too young.'

'Has she gone to Romford town centre with anyone?' I enquired.

'A bunch of girls from her school, I think.'

'You don't know?'

'No, but I do know that her virtue will be in tatters if we don't get her.'

The girl's mother was able to provide me with a photograph of her daughter.

'Wait here in my office, me and a colleague will go to

see if we can find her.'

A PC gave me a lift in the GP car to South Street where we found a cluster of groupies by the stage door of the Odeon. I showed some of them the photo and asked if they had seen the girl I was looking for.

Seeing that the police were looking for the girl, one tentative teenager pointed and said, 'She's gone inside.'

I went into the stage door where the security guards parted for me like the Red Sea.

The melodic harmony of *Massachusetts* pulsated through my body as I climbed a flight of concrete stairs leading to the artists' dressing room, where a young girl fitting Rachel's description stood. She looked a lot older than her years, a carbon copy of her mother.

'Rachel?' I mouthed.

I was now quite used to members of the public looking in disbelief when they were confronted by a young WPC, and Rachel was no different.

'Your mother has reported you missing and I am here to take you to Romford Police Station where she is waiting for you.'

With that the girl broke down.

'She never wants me to do anything, or go anywhere.' She sobbed.

Secretly I empathised with this teenager; what she was saying reminded me of my own upbringing and historic misdemeanours.

'But she didn't know where you were,' raising my voice a level, 'have you been in the dressing room with the group?'

'No, I was waiting for them to come off the stage after.'

'How did you get past the security?'

'One of the minders picked me out of the crowd and invited me up here.'

With that I knew I had reached the girl in time.

'Come along now. The show's over.'

So mother and daughter were reunited and the girl's details were kept on a most effective record at New Scotland Yard's A4 branch; an index formerly manned by women officers solely to record descriptions of juveniles who had come to the attention of police. Names, aliases, hair and eye colour - something that could not be changed – along with ages, addresses and any identifying marks or scars.

Women police gained a myriad of skills through the variety of different jobs that came their way, although none of the officers, male or female that I met in my service had psychology backgrounds. Common sense was more beneficial than any 'ology', and very few officers who joined had, or were expected to have, a degree in anything.

One of the many things we had to learn 'on the job' was how to pacify those persons of unsound mind who might have come to our attention. Warley, a Mental Hospital in the county of Essex, specifically comes to mind. It was close to the border with Havering, so quite often a police officer would be called upon to pick up an absconder and thereafter escort them in an ambulance or a police car back to where they had come.

The types of people I came upon demonstrated various mental conditions but quite often they had taken on delusions of grandeur.

'You realise officer I am Napoleon?' A middle aged man once announced. And then there was Margaret, by no means the famous Royal but she insisted that her sister

A Girl in Blue

Queen Elizabeth would be the one to take her back to Buckingham Palace.

In such cases, one quickly learnt that it was best to agree with these claims in order to avoid confrontation or any sudden outbursts of violence, for apart from the little judo I knew and the self-defence classes taught in training school, I was completely untrained for such encounters, able only to keep a cool head, trusting it to be the safest and most effective in any difficult situation.

Upminster railway station, where the District Line terminates, was the place to which police were often called by station staff to assist with all sorts of difficult situations, but mainly we would get called to anyone who was under the influence of drink and who had boarded the train somewhere on the underground, fallen asleep and ended up at the end of the line usually on the last train of the night. Depending on the condition of the individual, they could be arrested for being drunk and disorderly and kept in the police station overnight until they had sobered up and could face a magistrate.

If police happened to come across a drunk who was also in charge of a child apparently under the age of seven, then a female officer would be sent for to help with the arrest and if necessary arrange for the child to be put into the care of the social services.

*

The Traffic Patrol was stronger and contained more manpower in the 1960s than it did in later years, although the first female Traffic Patrol Officer, Dee O'Donoghue, was not appointed until 1977. However, in Havering traffic policing came in all sorts of guises and I regularly came upon drivers who had to be reported for having no

Policing Romford

road fund licence displayed, occasionally no insurance or other violations of traffic regulations. And since parking wardens did not arrive in Romford until about a year after I started, I was kept busy putting parking tickets on cars. As far as my superiors were concerned 'getting results' was successful policing, but having to deal with irate drivers was something I had to learn not to take personally.

The A127 road was constructed as a new road project in the 1920s to replace the old A13. It became known as the Southend Arterial Road, linking London and Southend-on-Sea and runs through Havering's ground. The very nature of the dual carriageway road led to frequent accidents so local officers were often called there.

On one occasion at around two o'clock in the afternoon I was with a PC in a light blue Morris 1100 Panda car. We were travelling east in the nearside lane, when we noticed a VW Beetle coming off a slip road ahead of us. But as it joined the A127, Trevor shouted: 'Bloody Hell, the driver's turned right onto the oncoming traffic and is coming straight toward us!'

The primary object of an efficient police quickly came to mind - the preservation of life!

Something had to be done and fast. East-bound cars in other lanes had to swerve out of the car's path to avoid a collision.

Trevor braked hard, and flashed the Panda's headlights.

Fortunately the VW stopped just in front of us, and we saw that it was being driven by an elderly female. But before we spoke to the driver I beckoned her to pull over onto the hard shoulder, whilst Trevor directed traffic away from the obstruction.

The woman was extremely shaken.

'I'm so sorry, I just wasn't thinking straight. My husband died recently and this is the first time since that I've been out on the road.'

After expressing our sympathies we gave the woman some necessary advice but had to caution and report her for driving without due care and attention. Mercifully, my colleague and I happened to be on the scene that day to prevent a possible pile up.

The 1967 Road Safety Act introduced the roadside breathalyser. This was made available to police forces across the country to legally enforce the maximum blood-alcohol level for drivers who exceeded the limit. So part of the ongoing career development for police officers was to attend a course on how to administer this testing equipment so as to be able to effectively test a driver for suspected drink-driving, and to make an arrest if the test proved positive.

And so, one summer evening while patrolling in Kilo 7, it happened. My driver Jack, a Class one driver, noticed a Mark 2 Cortina in front of us swerving from the nearside to the outside lane on Main Road.

'That driver looks the worse for wear,' I said.

'We'll get him to pull over.'

We indicated to the driver to stop but he failed to do so and raced ahead. The blue light on the Jag was activated and a chase ensued. With the skill of a Formula One driver Jack caught up with the Cortina, cut in front of it and both vehicles came to a sudden stop.

'Get out of the car,' Jack demanded.

Jack was usually a very courteous cop when dealing with the public, but on this occasion the driver was so incapable of moving let alone standing, that any politeness toward him would have been wasted. He didn't speak and stayed sitting in the driver's seat so I put into practise what I had been trained to do; I breathalysed and arrested him for being over the legal limit. He was also later charged with dangerous driving. In Court the result of the breathalyser test was produced and the offender duly fined.

There were sometimes incidents of stray cattle or horses found wandering along Essex roads, especially on the A127 which was bordered by farms and open fields.

A colleague and I were again out together one fine morning in a patrol car between Romford and Upminster. Our small talk about the fortieth birthday party his family was planning for him was suddenly interrupted.

'Kilo 5, Kilo 5 are you receiving me? Over.'

'Kilo 5 to KD yes we are receiving you. Over.'

'Police have been alerted to a stray horse seen on the eastbound carriageway of the A127. What is your position? Over.'

We explained to base where we were, and as it happened we soon saw that the traffic ahead of us had slowed considerably and the said animal was wandering from one side of the carriageway to the other. I had had no horse-handling experience, but my Essex country-born colleague assured me that he had. So we parked the police car on the hard shoulder, stopped the traffic and faced the problem.

'Now what we do,' Harry said, 'is to approach the horse and grab its mane, and if it runs, run in the same direction.'

I recalled the advice I had learnt in the Highways Act which lay down exactly as he suggested, 'Run in the same direction as the animal whilst holding on!'

The drivers of the cars that had been forced to stop were now growing impatient but appeared relieved to see police in attendance, but I began to feel somewhat worried about what we were expected to do. I knew it was best not to stand anywhere near the rear of a horse for fear of being kicked to death and there was no way I wanted to have the life crushed out of me by such a beast, but I was relieved to see that the creature was more pony-sized than a fully grown thoroughbred. However, it seemed just as nervous as I, so Harry gave me his next instruction.

'Right, when I count to three you grab one side and I'll grab the other, ready?'

'Ready'

'1, 2, 3.'

We grabbed the horse's mane as planned, ready to steer it clear of the road. The animal jerked forward and Harry lost his grip. I remained in charge but was left running down the outside lane of the dual carriageway hanging on for dear life. Leaping astride the animal bareback to slow it down would have looked most spectacular, but no way was I going to attempt that in a straight skirt and stockings. My hat flew off. Damn, I thought, I hope Crossy doesn't catch sight of me being improperly dressed for duty. She had a tendency to turn up at the most inconvenient times. Furthermore I knew I was running out of strength, but eventually even though I didn't know if it was the right thing to do or not, I did muster up enough breath to shout very loudly in the animal's ear.

'Whoa!'

Much to my surprise the horse suddenly stopped, so I pulled it over by its mane onto the central reservation, held on as firmly as possible with one hand and gently patted its neck with the other.

Having removed the obstruction, the waiting vehicles were able to move off safely. Drivers cheered and waved as they passed by. Then I saw Harry and his two bellies come panting towards me. He was holding my hat, rescued from under a once stationary car.

'Didn't we do well, never thought we'd sort that problem out so quick?'

I looked at him in dismay. It was not him that was covered in dust and dirt and smelling of something less becoming than my normal Chanel No. 5.

In due course the animal was taken to a local pound to await collection by its owner if indeed it had one. So such were the joys of patrolling the 'sticks'; a central London police woman would be highly unlikely to have to catch a runaway horse.

When a milk lorry shed its load of full glass bottles in Main Road right outside Romford police station I was called to the front office by the Station sergeant.

'Get yourself out there and direct the traffic!'

I had learnt how to stop or direct traffic whilst in training school. Stand tall, point the finger of your right hand directly at the driver of the vehicle and then hold up a flat hand to indicate that the vehicle must stop a procedure I often had to carry out when on duty but the milk lorry spillage was definitely the messiest.

Fatal road accidents were most often dealt with by Traffic Patrol officers, so I usually only got to know about the carnage afterwards during a refreshment break in the station canteen. But if I was personally involved it was mainly to help remove debris from the accident site, reduce congestion or direct traffic. Romford police all used a particular specialist vehicle recovery service that would reward officers for bringing business their way, otherwise known as a 'bung'. After one such accident on A127 a colleague came into the women police office to see me.

'Here's a fiver for you love. You did your bit out there. Couldn't leave you out.'

I was pleased to be included, but I won't admit whether I took the money or not, since I haven't been cautioned!

Late in March 1968 I arrived on duty and was told by the station sergeant to join the PCs in the parade room situated just next door to the women police office. The parade room was where PCs booked on fifteen minutes before the start of their shift, something women police never did so something serious was expected.

There the sergeant announced grimly:

'We have received news today that our Commissioner, Sir Joseph Simpson, has died at his home in Roehampton.'

The news was quite unexpected as 'Joe Soap', as he was referred by the common constable, was only 58 years of age. He had served as Commissioner for ten years and we later learned that his death was caused by overwork and stress, an understandable reason for his demise as he had been the instigator of several innovative investigative departments attached to Scotland Yard. His successor was Sir John Waldron whose appointment was assumed by many to be a temporary fill-in role, but circumstances such as a rise in police salaries and pensions, and the fall of the Labour government in 1970 saw Waldron stay on for several years longer than expected.

In June 1968 in nearby Dagenham, sewing machinists at the Ford Motor plant took strike action in support of their claim for regrading, parity with men in the

'C' grade and recognition of their skills. As with most demonstrations police had to be in attendance to prevent breaches of the peace, so during the three weeks the women were on strike I was sent to join other officers to do tours of duty there. There was little trouble as such, just women making their voices heard. But the strike was given a high profile when the whole plant was closed and Barbara Castle, the Employment Minister, was brought in to help negotiate a settlement. The women finally settled for 92% of the C grade rate and the whole incident paved the way for other women workers to fight for equality.

Late in the summer of 1968 I took my first holiday without my parents, something I could now afford to do independently, and chose to take a package holiday to Ibiza with Marilyn or Mandi as she later preferred to be known, my best friend from schooldays. The 1960s saw Ibiza start to boom with the 'flower power' revolution which saw stacks of forward-thinking hippies from across Europe descend on the Balearic island, attracted by its laid-back attitude, unspoilt natural beauty and its great weather. After nearly two years of training and having to grow up fast in a very responsible job, those two weeks away were just the break I needed.

In the winter of 1968, two fourteen-year-old girls who could not account for their movements were picked up one evening in Romford's South Street by two late turn PCs. Both girls were brought in to my office. One appeared more frightened than the other, but they were both cold and unkempt and had only a small bag of extra clothes and the grand sum of three pounds between them.

'Now girls, tell me what brings you to Romford?'

A Girl in Blue

'We just ended up here,' one of them replied in a mumbled tone.

Then the other girl added:

'We got a lift from a lorry driver.' I shuddered at the thought.

'Where do you live?' I asked.

'Why?' The girl with attitude who was determined not to answer any further questions, preferring to stuff her face full of the sandwiches I had ordered for them from the canteen.

'Because you failed to give your address to the officers who picked you up and now I need to know.'

The other girl weakened under pressure and cried, 'Wales.'

'Wales?' I echoed.

'Yes, Mountain Ash.'

'Do your parents know where you are?'

'No, we ran away without telling them.' Came the reply, choking back the tears.

'Well, best you tell me your names and addresses then we can let your parents know you are safe.'

'Bronwyn.'

'Bronwyn what?'

'Bronwyn Thomas.'

'Linda Williams,' the tearful one revealed her details more readily. 'What will happen to us?

As a result of what I had gleaned from the two girls, I explained that I would be contacting Havering's social services to arrange overnight accommodation for them. The Welsh police were also contacted, who informed me that the girls had been reported missing by their parents. The following day I took Bronwyn and Linda to

Romford Juvenile Court to outline how they had come to the attention of police and that they were in need of Care and Protection. The Court deferred the case to the girls' home town of Mountain Ash in the Cynon Valley, in the County Borough of Rhondda Cynon Taf. Later the same day two Welsh police officers came to the police station to escort the girls back home.

When a date for the hearing was arranged I was required to attend the Welsh Court to present my evidence. After a lengthy train journey from London I arrived in the small Welsh town. One of my colleagues, station sergeant Salter, came from Mountain Ash so he arranged for his mother to put me up overnight in her spare room. It was winter, mid-February, and the warm welcome I received from Mrs Salter did little to compensate for the complete lack of heating in the house. I have never been as cold in bed as I was that night. The following morning, a splash of icy water poured from a jug on the dressing table into a pink and white floral patterned wash basin chilled me further, but helped to revive me after what was a virtually sleepless night.

The Court I had to attend was nearby; a special Juvenile Court hearing was arranged just for my case in Aberdare. I arrived smartly dressed in the green and tan dress and coat I had worn to Crown Court during my training school days. There were no other cases that day so I was quickly invited by the Court usher to take the stand in front of the Magistrate sitting aloft at his bench, a portly Welshman somewhat resembling Mr Pickwick. He seemed intrigued to be in the presence of a police officer who had come all the way from London and he listened intently while I referred to the two girls concerned and related the facts to him.

Then, as I was about to leave the courtroom, he leaned

A Girl in Blue

forward:

'Officer, I wish to commend you on the work you have done to protect these youngsters, and also the way you have presented your case.'

The rewarding part about this job for me, as well as the comment from the Magistrate, was seeing that the two families were to receive support from the Social Services. But most of all it was very reassuring to see how relieved the girls were to be back at home again after their brush with the law. It had been a teenage prank they were unlikely to repeat in a hurry.

The following year the Upminster hostel was again fully occupied, with four women police officers in residence so as my 21st birthday neared I decided to make it a memorable one and invited close family, friends and colleagues to a party. CID officers with whom we worked often invited me or other single WPCs to their social events, perhaps to a party in one of the market traders large detached houses in neighbouring Noak Hill, or for drinks in local pubs, so on the occasion of my birthday it was good to have the opportunity to reciprocate. I wore my long hair up in securely-fastened ringlets, and sported a newly-purchased black cat-suit with chain belt which I had purchased from Richards shop in Romford. For one night only that February 2nd, the walls of the Hostel reverberated with the sound of music and laughter. Even the on duty PCs from the station next door didn't want to miss out on the action.

During quiet spells in a police station WPCs could sometimes be deployed in the Communications room, or 'Comms' as it was called, to man the switchboard when the civilian telephonist was having a break. I had no actual training on how to do this, but from time to time I had observed one or other of the two middle-aged operators, Marg and Edna, and quickly learnt how to make a telephone connection by placing the relevant cord into the required socket. Answering calls and putting the caller through to a particular department was interesting enough, but moreover proved to be a welcome opportunity to relieve one's patrol weary feet.

Comms was always very busy. In one corner was the switchboard and in the other stood a teleprinter, a noisy device that constantly transmitted telegraph messages and printed messages received on a constant roll of perforated paper. The dedicated teleprinter was eventually made obsolete in police stations by, in turn, the fax machine, then personal computer, inkjet printer, broadband and the internet.

One day in the summer of 1968 while I was manning the switchboard a handsome police Cadet walked in. He had arrived at Romford in order to gain experience of working at a station before going to do his thirteen weeks training at Hendon.

He was immaculately turned out. His toe-capped boots shone like glass, and his dark blue uniform trousers had the sharpest pressed creases down the front of each of his legs that supported his six foot frame. His uniform shirt of glazed blue cotton was pristine and he had immaculate well-groomed dark brown curly hair. I was immediately smitten; my relationship with Graham had recently paled into insignificance due to the geographical distance between us so it was mutually agreed that our engagement should end.

On seeing Charlie, I was determined to give him a guided tour of the station. For me, it was a case of love at first sight and it was not long before we became inseparable, although being a cadet he was allowed to live at home with his parents in Chingford.

When he reached his 18th birthday I was invited to a party held in his honour in private rooms above a café owned by Charlie's French grandmother in Swallow Street, just off Regent Street.

Chas, Charlie's father, was a Londoner born and bred with the same East End swagger as his son. He was a self-made man, originally an orphan, who owned dry cleaners in Walthamstow. I soon came to know why Charlie had such well-pressed clothes!

On my arrival at the party I received welcoming embraces from his close family, kisses on both cheeks and was introduced.

'Son, you're telling me porkies, surely she's not a copper. You've got yourself one of those fashion models.'

The way I had been regarded by Chas was quite flattering, as my style was in fact fashioned on sixties model icon Twiggy: a blue mini shift dress, white tights and patent shoes, although unlike her blonde bob my hair was brown, long and straight to my waist. Both Charlie's parents seemed to like me, particularly his mother Vivienne.

'Mon dieu, I am so pleased Sharlie has met someone like you. Un couple parfait.'

And I believed her son would be with me forever.

*

A young person who frequently came to the attention of Romford police was a girl about four years younger than I was at that time. We shall call her Jenny. She was frequently arrested for being under the influence of drink or in possession of drugs. She lived on the Harold Hill

Policing Romford

council estate which had been conceived as part of the Greater London Plan in 1944 as a satellite town on the edge of Romford.[6]

Whenever Jenny came into the station she was unkempt, and went from being a juvenile to adult offender with an ever-growing list of convictions. I wasn't surprised to read about her years later, discovering that she had ended up in Holloway Prison for fraud offences. While there Jenny befriended Myra Hindley, and came up with a plan to escape.

'That's what I would do in your position,' explained Jenny. 'You'll die in here otherwise.' The idea began to take hold in Hindley's mind. But where would they go? Abroad; Jenny could get hold of passports, visas and cash. Some people on the outside owed her favours. It was a mad idea, but it nagged away at Hindley. It seemed the only chance she and her prison warder lover had of living together. The more she thought about freedom, the more impossible the idea of a life without it felt.

The plan was to flee over Holloway's perimeter wall using a ladder, drive to Heathrow in a hired car and take the 'very convenient' 11.00pm flight to Rio. Once there, they would enquire about missionary work. Hindley's lover went along with the plan, seeing it as another of her fantasies. But then it turned from a fantasy into a reality. They got as far as making an impression of the prison's master key and posting it to a forger. But there was an alert on at the time about IRA parcel bombs, and the suspicious package was intercepted. The police

---

6   Land was purchased in 1947 by the London County Council in recognition of the urgency of housing required after the end of the Second World War; building started in the following year and was completed in 1958, with more than 7,500 homes built which would house 25,000 people.

descended on Holloway and the escape was foiled.

Many a young person like Jenny came to the attention of women police, for a variety of reasons. They had either been arrested for an offence, were in need of care and protection or had been reported missing by their parents or carers. There were times when a young person had been sexually assaulted, raped or involved in underage sex. In any of these cases, the Divisional Surgeon would be called to the police station to carry out a physical examination of the woman or young person in order to gather evidence.

One fifteen-year-old girl we shall call Tracy who came to my attention was proven to have had sex while underage. She had been associating with an older man, who would have been charged but he was ultimately able to prove that he believed the girl was over 16. Unlike another fourteen-year-old girl I had dealings with who insisted:

'We only did it once, and now I'm pregnant.'

But after being interviewed by me she admitted for several months she had been freely associating with a married man and since she was under the age of consent, the offender had to be arrested.

Tracy did in fact look a lot older than her years but since her promiscuity had come to the attention of police, I took her to Havering Juvenile Court for a decision to be made about her care. She was a lippy individual announcing that she would go back to her boyfriend 'as soon as I am finished with you fucking rozzers.' However, at the start of proceedings she was reduced to a timid youngster and when she was asked to take the Bible in her right hand and take the oath shakily she read it out.

'The evidence I shall give will be the truth, the whole

truth and nothing but the truth.' The Magistrate heard the evidence from police and other witnesses, and then an interim decision had to be made.

'What will happen now?' sobbed the girl's mother.

'Your daughter's case will be looked into by the Probation Service.'

A slim bespectacled woman in her mid-forties came forward. She smiled at the girl.

'I know this has all been upsetting for you and your mother, but until we compile our reports we will not know how to deal with you, so in the meantime you will be taken to a Remand Home.'

'A Remand Home? For how long?' the mother asked.

'A month.'

Now in custody, the girl was put in the care of the Court matron, a motherly Irish lady of advancing years named Bridget, to await transportation to the Remand Home. Then it was my job to escort the girl there in the back of a police car.

The PC allocated to drive us into the Essex countryside was familiar with the route from Romford to Great Baddow. The journey was only about 24 miles away, but for the girl who feared the unknown it seemed endless as we travelled together, further and further into deepest Essex. The silence was somewhat deafening, so I spoke:

'Like you, this will be the first time I've been to Great Baddow.'

'I've had to take a few here before,' the PC chipped in, 'Newport House, has been a Remand Home for girls since 1945, not that I've being going there since then of course.'

I smiled. The girl continued to look glumly at the road ahead while the PC continued to air his knowledge.

A Girl in Blue

'The House was purchased at the turn of the century by Ernest Dossetor, a stockbroker from Sevenoaks in Kent, and he lived there until his death in 1944. Afterwards the House was purchased from Ernest's son by Chelmsford County Council and converted into a Remand Home for girls.'

That said, eventually the car turned into a long winding road called Molrams Lane, and the old House, tucked away and surrounded by woodland, came into view.

When we stopped on the front drive of the house our driver sounded his horn. A moment later the cheery-faced, grey-haired matron appeared with a small dog lapping at her heels. As we got out of the car the girl looked up into my eyes and grabbed my arm tightly.

'Please don't leave me here,' she said. But after a few reassuring words she was uncuffed and I handed her over into the care of Miss Scrivens, and my driver and I returned to Romford. I discovered later that my frightened little girl had received two years' probation for her own protection.

Newport House was somewhere I would visit several more times, sometimes driving myself there, during my service on K Division, either to deliver or collect a young female. Later, in the 1970s, it was closed and given a new identity as a conference centre.

Our work in the sticks compared to that of WPCs in central London was a far better experience than I or my female colleagues expected it to be. We discovered a varied socio-economic mix on our sub-division, from council estates to suburban housing and to Gidea Park a small predominantly affluent residential area originally known as Romford Garden Suburb constructed between 1910–11 as an exhibition of town planning and where

Policing Romford

several celebrities of the day resided. Women police could be called to domestic violence incidents where, as long as there had not been an assault committed, a warning, especially by a female officer, was often enough to diffuse most volatile situations. After having attended any incident, pocket book notes always had to be made to record the day, date, time and place of everything that had happened.

One particular misdeed which I could never manage to turn a blind eye to in Romford town centre was if I saw anyone, particularly kids, riding their bikes on the footway. It wasn't something that just annoyed me as of course it was a violation of a local by-law. So I would shout after them, 'If you're old enough to ride a bike, you're old enough to ride it on the road!' In general my response would fall on deaf ears, but I felt all the better for having said it and sometimes if possible I would report the offender.

The Litter Act of 1958 was a particular favourite of mine, for if saw people dropping litter in the street, like the riding a bike on the pavement, my hackles would rise. For flagrant offences I would have had great delight in reporting the offender but if I called out 'Put it in the bin!' now I would more than likely be worse off for doing so.

After I had been at Romford a couple of years a woman police Inspector arrived, so Crossy was no longer totally in charge of her flock and she would have to answer to the superior officer Honor Miles. In fact I got on well with her. She turned out to be very supportive and from the start quickly made an assessment of her officers. As for me, she remarked one day:

'If you fell in a coalhole, my dear I am sure you would

come up smelling of roses!'

Little did she know that after climbing into a truck in the local coalyard on one of my first assignments, I had smelt and looked far less than rosy but I appreciated her opinion. I always tried to present myself with a high degree of professionalism, but early on in my career I had no idea about how many times I would be covered in spit, blood, dirt or vomit.

Throughout my career I had to be prepared for the unexpected. One moment I could be in the women police office writing reports, and the next called to assist with an enquiry somewhere on the division. On one occasion I was called to assist with an incident at a house in Harold Hill. A woman had committed suicide and there were young children on the premises. On my arrival there was already of flurry of police activity, both uniform and plainclothes officers, as well as the SOCO (Scenes of Crime Officer), all jostling on the narrow flight of stairs to the first floor of the three-bedroom council house. As I walked into the hallway I felt my shoes sticking to the mock-tiled lino, and I was met by the unpleasant aroma of stale chips and urine. The woman's two young children, aged about two and four, were in the living room with the neighbour who had called at the house a couple of hours earlier. But, getting no answer from the mother and hearing the children crying, she alerted police.

Although fellow officers did not want me to witness the scene I felt it was something I had to assess for myself and I was allowed past the officer guarding the door of the bathroom. The white-tiled walls were crimson-splattered, and the lifeless body of a fair-haired woman was lying in a bath of similarly-coloured water. I knew then that my specific job was to make arrangements for the children to be looked after by a close relative, while the CID led the investigation.

A few days later I met one the CID officers in the nick.

'Did the woman on Harold Hill's ground top herself?'

'Well, the postmortem ruled out foul play, and we did find a scribbled suicide note in the bedroom she shared with her boyfriend.'

'The father of her kids?'

'No, he is inside for attempted murder.'

'Who had he tried to kill?'

'The lady in the bath.'

'The note?'

'Well, it appears her boyfriend, who she thought she'd found happiness with, was planning to go back to his own wife and children so she threatened to take her life.'

'So basically it was a cry for help that went too far?'

'Sure. She might have stood a chance if she'd taken a few too many aspirin, but slashing your wrists with a sharpened carving knife is pretty effective.'

She thought she wanted to die, but in reality she just wanted to be saved.

1969-70
Hendon Driving School

Although I had been taught a little about driving by Douglas and subsequent boyfriends, I had never had the opportunity to take private driving lessons. But after my two year probation period, Inspector Miles allowed me to put in a formal application to my Superintendent for a police driving course at Hendon, a world-renowned elite driving school, where even Royals had been taught to drive. So without much ado my request was granted, and every day for five weeks I made the long return journey to Hendon.

The driving principle at Hendon was based on 'Roadcraft', a system introduced in 1956 following principles set out by the Metropolitan police to improve driving standards. The driving instructors, all police officers with advanced driving qualifications, lectured on practical car maintenance and the theory of road safety, but the *piece de resistance* for me was to get to drive on the skid pan. Driving on a prepared slippery road surface enabled all the students to practise control of skidding, but as much as it was a very exhilarating experience, it was such an important part of learning to drive safely.

Since I had never looked under the bonnet of a car and knew not one end of a carburetor from the other, I soon became engrossed with the theory of mechanics. I learnt how to check the fuel, lights, water and the electrics and how to change vehicle tyres.

Novice drivers were taught to follow a simple 'drill', or sequence of events, carrying out a manoeuvre, mirror, signal or brake whereby a driver could ensure that his vehicle was always in the right place at the right time, travelling at the right speed and in the correct gear. A driver would therefore learn to be in complete control of a vehicle in any situation.

Another part of the course taught drivers how to verbalise road conditions. At first one felt rather self-conscious doing so but after realising that saying, for example, 'There is a pedestrian crossing ahead.' or 'the vehicle in front is indicating to turn right.' or 'there is a school road sign and a child on the nearside kerb playing with a ball,' the procedure all made perfectly good sense.

The various vehicles I was introduced to had unsynchronized manual transmission, so the method of 'double de-clutching' had to be mastered. Instead of pushing the clutch in once and shifting directly to another gear, the driver first engages the transmission in neutral before shifting to the next gear. The clutch is pressed and released with each change, something that quite out of habit I was apt to do quite unnecessarily when driving more modern cars.

Part of the Driving School course fell on 21st July 1969 when a four-hour night drive was arranged; a circular trip from the Hendon, through the adjacent county of Hertfordshire and back. For more than one reason, this drive became to be a most memorable one, for not only was driving at night a unique experience, but en-route my instructor and I listened to the radio and heard Apollo II and its three-man crew land on the Moon.

As my course progressed, it was not without its incidents. During another drive out with an instructor from Hendon in an unmarked blue Hillman, accompanied by two other trainees, I was driving along a dual carriageway en-route to Worthing, when I lost concentration and collided with the central reservation causing the car to overturn.

During the course, the importance of concentration had to be learnt by heart. It was actually drummed into us for it was considered to be at the very core of good driving.

'Concentration is the application of mind and body to a particular endeavour with the complete exclusion of anything not relevant to that endeavour.'

Throughout our journeys none of us ever wore seatbelts (seat belt legislation was not passed until 1983), but in this instance as we began to rotate, with great presence of mind, the instructor in the passenger seat threw up his legs and jammed me between the soles of his boots and the driver's door. Fortunately none of us was hurt, but we all ended upside down and had to crawl out of the windows on to the grass verge. Following correct procedures in the case of any accident involving a driving school vehicle, the Driving School Superintendent at Hendon was immediately informed. Naturally he was none too happy about the damage incurred, but since none of us was injured a replacement vehicle and a driver were duly dispatched to transport us all back to base.

The end of the course culminated in the standard driving test and I managed to pass the course. However, my final report read as follows:

'WPC Willoughby has a tendency to fall into bad

habits, but it is hoped that she will maintain the standard reached.'

So although very embarrassing, I had got away with my mishap and I was awarded a Metropolitan police 'Class 5' Driving certificate.

Having passed the standard driving course, back at my station I was authorised to drive some of the police vehicles. I really enjoyed driving so a liberating chapter in my career began. Previously I had had to rely on lifts from other police drivers to take me to my enquiries, but now I could drive the Morris 1000 Panda car, the Hillman General Purpose car and the Station van. I would have liked to have been able to drive the fast-response Rover, but to do so drivers had to complete a Class 1 driving course and I was not ready for that. I did, however, have to become more aware of routines that previously I had little interest in. Such as where police vehicles were garaged, who the civilian mechanics were that maintained them. I also needed to know which designated petrol stations to use and how the acquisition of petrol had to be recorded in the vehicle's fuel log book.

The Panda cars were the vehicles I mainly had access to. They were introduced in 1965, registered to New Scotland Yard, and in service with the Metropolitan Police from September 1969 until June 1971. In many areas the Panda replaced the traditional 'Bobby on the beat', when it was considered that larger suburban or rural areas could be more effectively patrolled by officers in cars as opposed to being on foot, bicycles or motorcycles. Needless to say, the Panda had its limitations but whenever there was a 'shout for back-up' on the two-way radio I would put my foot flat down on the accelerator to get to colleagues who required assistance and hope for the best. Cars also provided shelter from the weather, but in contrast to the

Hendon Driving School

benefits of patrolling in cars their installation came at a cost, in some ways distancing the police from the public.

Driving was an essential requirement for us women in the hostel, so one by one we managed to purchase our own cars. Tish was a car enthusiast and the first to buy her own. Then, being the kind-hearted soul she was, she would occasionally offer me a lift to get to work rather than my having take the bus into Romford.

> If it is still foggy and cold, wake me up and I'll run you in as the fog was bad in parts. If you're up early there's a 'News of the Screws' downstairs to catch up with all the scandal! -Tish.

I was also keen to buy a car of my own. If a secondhand car dealer couldn't be found in Romford then one couldn't be found anywhere. So, following reliable recommendations from colleagues I went to look at a red Hillman Imp which was for sale in one of those afore mentioned posh houses in Gidea Park. It was a 'B' registration, 1964 model, was just about the right engine size for a newly-qualified lady driver and at £200 a price I could afford.

My car gave me so much independence, enabling me to travel home on my days off to see my family in south London. However, it wasn't the most reliable, so there were times when I had to fix what turned out to be a recurring fault – a broken throttle cable. But I suppose with the car being five years old at the point of purchase I should have suspected its reliability would be in question. Still it got me about but on a soiree to the narrow streets of Soho, I unwittingly parked facing the wrong way in a one-way street. When I returned to my beloved Imp I discovered it had been towed away to the police compound at Vauxhall. Luckily I knew the sergeant on duty there, so after accepting my profound apologies he kindly released my car without charge; a lesson learned about where not to park!

1970-71
West End Central: Vice Squad

Having now successfully completed my two years' probation period I was free to take promotion, join specialist departments at New Scotland Yard or take a ten-week CID course. Promotion didn't appeal to me, but I did apply for - and got - a three-month tour of duty on the Vice Squad. This Squad was established in 1932 as the C Division Clubs and Vice Unit, later to become better known as the 'Clubs Office'. It was based on the third floor of West End Central Police Station (CD), in Savile Row, London W1 a crucial location as nearby Soho has been the most famous red light district in the United Kingdom since the mid-19th century.

Initially, under the Street Offences Act of 1959, the Squad primarily dealt with prostitution but later on nightclubs, gaming and casinos were included in their work. Westminster City Council supplied the gaming licences but if unlicensed clubs committed offences against the Act then it was the police who would carry out the investigations and planned raids.

During the Sixties, armed with improved technology, the Squad's focus moved onto criminal activity to include drugs, criminal control of clubs and brothels and the obscene publications industry. Plainclothes observations in such shady back-street establishments or even licensed premises were carried out by any of the team of about twenty men, and one WPC seconded from a division in the Metropolitan Police District. The Squad was led by a permanent senior officer. For each assignment the whole team would be briefed to discuss the dangers involved in carrying out observations and no officer, and never alone, would be allowed to enter suspect premises without the authorisation of the Superintendent. In later years, undercover officers (known as 'undies' in criminal circles) were subjected to psychological tests to ensure they could cope with the extreme demands and danger involved, but in my day no such support existed.

Most tours of duty on the Vice Squad started late at night and often continued into the early hours of the morning. Generally, casual observations would be made by any of the team acting as punters at target addresses. The task of undercover police was to gain as much evidence as possible and report back to senior officers, who would decide whether or not the premises should be raided. Once granted the squad officers would have an initial briefing and then a couple of other undercover officers would have to gain entry although this could be difficult at some premises, as there would be heavies on the door to vet the guests. So police officers on the Squad were chosen for their appearance, and soon learned to adopt ways of behaviour to enable access into central London clubs.

A few days into this new tour of duty, late as expected, I was told to report to the squad in West End Central's office with the rest of my colleagues. The prospect of being involved in under cover work of this nature was eagerly anticipated and when we were all assembled the Governor gave us the low down.

'We have gathered sufficient information to carry out a raid tonight in the Gargoyle strip club in Dean Street. It's all systems go.'

I knew a warrant to enter the club, known as Nell Gwynne by day and the Gargoyle Club at night would already have been obtained from a Magistrate on written information sworn by the informant i.e. a senior officer.

'What's it likely to be?' I asked a colleague.

'Disorderly conduct,' he replied.

The Super continued:

'At night Strippers have been seen performing overtly explicit acts, so I want you, Willoughby and Jeff, to get yourselves into the Club and, at the pre-determined time, get the doors open to let in the troops.'

Having Jeff with me was reassuring, for although he was in his early twenties, he was an experienced officer who had passed his Sergeant's exam after only a few years in the Job and was keen as mustard to carry out seedy assignments and had grown a beard and long curly hair especially for undercover work.

It was a hot night when we left by the back door of the police station. Jeff, dressed in blue jeans and a tie-dye shirt and I in an almost indecent leather mini skirt, knee high white boots and a loose muslin top adorned with tiny mirrors that reflected the lights of Carnaby Street as we passed through on our way to the planned destination. On arrival at the club we managed to get past the heavies on the door and after descending a flight of stairs to the basement area we sat ourselves on hard wooden chairs in the small dingy, smoke-filled auditorium facing the stage, which was just large enough to allow the performers to move around.

Two sleazy strippers came out and performed lukewarm

A Girl in Blue

acts, which did little to liven up any of the dozen or so men in the audience. In the meantime, Jeff and I needed to look like a couple so I leant affectionately on him whilst he leered impressively at the strippers, then all we had to do was to wait for the final act. According to previous observations that had been carried out there by squad officers, my colleague and I knew that it was the one to watch.

The stripper was a tall, topless, lavishly-made up brunette with hair that cascaded in silky ringlets about her shoulders. Her pale skin and somewhat small breasts glistened under the single spotlight as she gyrated and thrust a tiny strategically-placed array of sequins, seriously predating the vajazzle. At one point she stepped down cautiously from the stage in six-inch stilettos and paraded in front of the men sitting in the front row, stopping now and then to fondle them. One fat, middle-aged bald punter took the stripper's hand and plunged it on to his erect penis. Bingo! All was going to plan, so at the pre-determined time I made my way upstairs implying I was feeling a little faint in the heat but opened the front door to the raiding party. The dingy theatre filled with police officers and I was told by the inspector in charge to go on the stage and seize the main attraction. I took the performer by the arm, stating: 'I am a police officer. You are under arrest,' to which a deep voice responded: 'Alright Love, it's not the first time I've been nicked.'

He was a transvestite!

Gerrard Street in Soho was famed for its many basement Chinese gaming clubs, whose customers played Pai Gow and Fan-Tan; Mahjong was also played by the more elderly punters but never for money; perhaps something can be said for being older and wiser. Not having any

West End Central: Vice Squad

oriental-looking officers on the Squad, evidence was hard to come by although each club had an English-speaking minder who was able to liaise with police officers when they did visit such premises. If a raid was considered necessary in a Chinese establishment because gaming laws were being flouted, I learnt that the owners took little notice of the consequences for afterwards, gaming tables would be disassembled by police and removed, only to be replaced hours later.

The Playboy club was operational at the time, and although not under particular surveillance officers from the Vice Squad would often frequent its glamorous interior and wonder at the waitresses in their scanty bunny costumes, inspired by the tuxedo-wearing Playboy rabbit mascot. While socialising there my colleagues and I got to know Victor Lownes, an American who, on behalf of club founder Hugh Hefner, headed Playboy Europe. He was Britain's highest-paid executive, eventually becoming Playboy Enterprise's second-biggest shareholder. Whilst overseeing the London gaming casino in the 1960s, it became Playboy's most successful business and to keep it that way Lownes was more than happy to encourage police officers on the premises. And we were more than happy to enjoy the experience, rubbing shoulders with celebrities and wealthy customers.

The Colony Room, otherwise known as 'Muriels' after its formidable hostess Muriel Belcher, was another Soho club that Jeff and I were directed by our superior officer to get ourselves inside to see what was going on.

As often was the case, it was approaching midnight when we left the police station in Savile Row. The premises, in Dean Street, were a fifteen-minute walk away. There was no-one on the door to check who we might be, so we accessed the first floor venue via a

A Girl in Blue

grubby narrow staircase. The club's interior smelt of cigarettes and stale perfume, but what made me more nauseous were the sickly green walls painted with fronds of bamboo. The mottled mirrors, leopard-skin barstools and plastic tropical plants completed the tasteless decor.

During our briefing back at the nick we were told that the premises might be enlivened by the antics of regular customer Francis Bacon and his crowd of 'vino veritas' cronies, people more likely to speak the truth when drunk. But having no idea who Francis Bacon was, neither Jeff nor I identified any such patron.

However, the Colony's real claim to fame in the good old days of strict licensing hours was that it would sell drinks when other places couldn't - a haven for hardened drinkers. Jeff and I enjoyed a couple of hours, chatting with some of the other customers while purchasing drinks from the bar. At that time I only ordered Scotch and American, Scotch whisky in a rocks glass topped with Schweppes dry ginger ale, a drink that I would make last for as long as possible. I never once witnessed anyone on the squad being under the influence of alcohol, as having gone through a strict selection process they were officers committed to their duties. But when they were off duty most officers did frequent their local as an escape from the rigours of the job.

But as for the Colony Club, when we were confident there was sufficient evidence that licensing laws were being breached and offences being committed, we left the premises to report back to base and were once more in the midst of Soho nightlife. Red lights were everywhere - in the upstairs windows of buildings - and every other entrance led to a strip club, massage parlour, private cinemas showing blue movies or sex shops selling magazines and 8mm home movies, all likely targets for police, but on that occasion left for another time.

Ronnie Scott's Jazz Club at 47 Frith Street was another Soho club that Vice Squad officers visited, often more for social reasons rather than breaches of licensing laws. But the club was a good place to observe visiting clientele, either in the public area or in the private lounge, a room filled with wall-to-wall foam-filled cube-shaped cushions, like a child's softplay centre, but instead of being made of plastic they were velvet-covered with walls of matching crimson. Punters could lounge, drink and listen to the jazz or blues piped from the floor below.

Clubs Office also dealt with prostitutes, the likes of which came under the jurisdiction of the Street Offences Act 1959. Most offenders, who could be as diverse and unusual as one might expect, when seen to be loitering or soliciting in the street or public place for the purpose of prostitution were initially cautioned. After a second caution they could be arrested without warrant. Police would always be interested to find out who 'Toms', as they were known by were working for. The pimp–prostitute relationship was, and still can be, widely understood to be abusive and controlling, although some women did manage to work independently.

After a known seventeen year old prostitute, who shall be known as Heather, was eventually arrested, I interviewed her about how she came to be working on the streets. Speaking in a soft Scottish brogue she explained.

'At fifteen I ran away from home to the bright lights of London, where I tried to get a job in a coffee shop or café.'

'Did you?'

'No, I was sleeping rough for a few weeks.'

'How did you get into prostitution?'

'One day I met this good-looking guy who told me that my auburn hair made me extra attractive. He told me I had potential.'

'Why did you trust him?'

'He seemed kind, and as I was running out of money I thought he might help me find a job.'

'Then what happened?'

'He took me to a big house and let me have one of the rooms. There were other girls there too so I felt ok about it. A little while later he told me to buy some sexy clothes like the other girls wore.'

'Did he give you money to buy new clothes and make-up?

'Aye.'

'Then what happened?'

'He got me working the streets of Soho. From 7pm till sunrise.'

'Did he threaten you if you didn't do what he wanted?'

'Aye.'

As I got to know more about women who 'were on the game', I learnt that they often found themselves being preyed upon by criminals of robbery, theft or rape, who were kept more or less voluntarily by prostitutes for the sake of protection.

'So two years working for him?'

'Aye. He used to follow any of us girls around at night while we were working the streets.'

'Now that you've been arrested we can help you.'

'I hope so. I've probably had more than a hundred men. Although lost count really because I've been in a situation I haven't been able to escape. Not many girls on the game are doing it by cos they want to.'

'It's a very dangerous game.'

On this occasion Heather was not charged but she was put in touch with a support group. She revealed the name and address of her ponce and he was subsequently traced by undercover officers and charged with the offence of living off immoral earnings.

The Sexual Offences Act 1956 included sections making brothel-keeping an offence, so when observing such establishments police officers would have to pay particular attention to who and what type of people were using the premises. That is whether women were known to police, whether they were seen to be in the company of different men and how entry was gained to the suspect property. This would mean observations had to be carried out from a plainclothes vehicle or as close to the targeted property as possible. Sometimes, observations could be carried out by police officers from a good vantage point inside private addresses whose owners were more than happy to assist. Once again, when sufficient evidence had been gathered and officers were satisfied that offences were being committed arrangements would be made for the establishment to be raided.

In preparation for this next venture, I and the squad were briefed as usual:

'We've managed to get the front door key copied so this afternoon the raid is on.'

Once the briefing was over we set off to South Audley Street, in London's prestigious Mayfair, and arrived at the target address. The officer in charge used the duplicate key to open the door of the impressive-looking house and ten of us stormed the premises as planned, spreading out and beginning our search.

In a room on the first floor myself and another officer entered one of the bedrooms where we interrupted a prostitute astride a trouserless punter. My colleagues found clients in other bedrooms, so more than enough evidence was collected by police to enable the landlord to be prosecuted for running a brothel, so he was duly arrested and charged at West End Central police station.

The experience I gained on the Vice Squad was exceptional, and even though my influential brother-in-law was able to extend my tenure for a further three months I did eventually have to return to Division.

1971
Hornchurch Manor

During my absence from Division, my police Cadet boyfriend had become a fully-fledged police officer, and at nineteen he had been posted elsewhere in the Metropolitan Police District. Although I tried to keep the romance alive, I was heartbroken when I discovered that he had suddenly become engaged to a young woman he had met in the course of his work.

Furthermore, as soon as I was back at Romford I was informed that from then on my Manor was to be Hornchurch, a small town nestled between Upminster and Romford. As the only female police officer at the station I faced a new challenge, which helped to lessen the pain of losing Charlie, but for almost a year I lamented his loss.

At Hornchurch I had my own office and worked the usual women police shift pattern. There I was very much in control of my own day-to-day duties, patrolling the town on foot to establish relationships with the proprietors of the local stores whilst raising the public's awareness of my existence.

As well as all the usual demands made of a woman officer, my duties could include covering any of the school-crossing patrols, particularly if a regular lollipop lady was indisposed, or being called to detain a shoplifter in the supermarket or one of the other High Street stores.

The Hornchurch-based WPC also had to cover Upminster, as the police station there never had its own regular WPC although any of us female officers on the sub-division could be called there if our specialism was required. One day I happened to be on foot patrol in one of the High Street of Upminster, when I was suddenly confronted by a woman whose child had been bitten by a dog.

'Officer, please help,' the mother said whilst holding a man-sized bloodsoaked handkerchief over the young girl's nose 'the animal just went for her.'

I radioed for an ambulance whilst the mother tried to calm her daughter, who was obviously very shocked. I asked the bystanders if they had seen what happened but the girl answered.

'I only tried to stroke it,' she cried. So I continued to talk to her about anything and everything to take her mind off the situation until the medics arrived. The dog in question was a small terrier so as it happened it did not belong to one of the dangerous dog breeds, but on seeing the severity of the girl's injury it was necessary for me to report the dog's owner for not keeping the animal under control. This incident was all in a days work but made me aware of how unpredictable any dog can be.

Whilst in Hornchurch a good deal of my job involved the children who lived in St Leonard's, a children's home in Hornchurch Road. This establishment, formerly known as Hornchurch Children's Home, was built in 1889 by the poor-law guardians of the parish of St. Leonard, Shoreditch and according to records was designed by the architect FJ Smith. It was intended as an

Hornchurch Manor

improvement on the typical barracks-type residence, and comprised of eleven 'cottages', each able to accommodate thirty children who were either orphans or children that had, for various reasons, been put into care by the social services.

On the 80-acre site there was a school, workshops, a bakery, a swimming bath, an infirmary and out buildings. It was extended between 1893 and 1895, and then in 1930 the Home was taken over by the London County Council. Two years before I arrived, the site was acquired by the London Borough of Tower Hamlets from where all the children originated. From time to time those who were reported missing to police were often found to be heading back to their London roots. So the necessary alerts and descriptions were then circulated and usually absconders were picked up by police within a few hours.

After returning from the West End, due to the experience I had gained there and being the only female officer from K Division who had completed a tour of Clubs Office, I found that my fame had sufficiently spread to neighbouring divisions. So at one time, I was called away from Hornchurch to assist Stoke Newington CID with an undercover drugs raid in a club on their manor, a club whose clientele was mainly African and Caribbean, a quite different learning curve for me. The Ilford CID also asked if I could assist them with a planned raid at the Palais in the centre of Ilford where, when it happened, skinheads and reggae girls in hot pants abruptly ceased gyrating to Motown music as uniform police stormed in.

Other duties, most often given over to WPCs to deal with in the 1960s, were known as Home Office Alien Enquiries. These entailed visiting addresses to check the documents of immigrants mostly from the Indian subcontinent although often lumped together as one group by white Britons. These newcomers actually came from a variety of backgrounds, including Hindus from the Gujarat region of western India, Sikhs from the eastern Punjab region and Muslims from both the west part of Pakistan and East Pakistan. Following any discoveries I made, a detailed report had to be drawn up and submitted to my superior officer, and thereafter returned to the Home Office for a decision to be made regarding the person or the family's right to stay in the country.

As far as female CID officers were concerned, there were only a couple of them on K Division so they only came to my attention if they were in the station to help investigate a murder or serious sex offence. But in general, written statements from women or children who had been subjected to some sort of sexual offence could be taken by a uniformed police officer, who would thoroughly investigate the case to get the whole picture before deciding whether to 'write it off', as some male CID officers were sometimes known to do with a 'she asked for it' attitude. I believed that the responsibility involved in the investigation of such cases weighed heavily, for on the one hand there is the vital necessity for getting full and exact facts, and on the other the equal importance of doing so with the least possible distress to the victim.

Mothers of young victims were often greatly relieved if a woman officer called at the house to investigate a sexual offence that had come to light within the family home.

'If I'd known a lady police would call, I'd have complained about it long ago,' was a not unusual response.

On more than one occasion I was deployed in civvies

as a decoy to entrap 'a flasher'- the regular term then for a man who exposed his genitals in public. A park being the usual place where such an offence was committed, so with all such jobs I was briefed by a sergeant or inspector about the reported crime.

'We have had several reports from women about a middle-aged man exposing himself to them near the children's playground in Harrow Lodge park.'

'What's his description?'

'White. About 50 years of age, five foot eight, slim build, dark hair, balding.'

'Dress?'

'Believe it or not, the usual!'

'A mac?'

'You got it.'

'What if he does it?'

'Swap your handbag from one shoulder to the other and we will swoop.'

So to the designated area I would be sent, hoping of course that all the other officers were well secreted, while at the same time able to keep me well in their sights. These types of assignments usually resulted in a straightforward arrest, although there were cases of WPCs being attacked by men before the backup arrived.

Police were frequently called to Romford stores to arrest shoplifters for the offence known as our 'Bread and butter' duties. Theft from shops was a regular occurrence. The main departmental stores in the town at that time were Stones, Fine Fare and Marks and Spencer. All had their own store detectives who had good relationships with local police, and descriptions of potential thieves were exchanged or circulated on the telephone.

If a shoplifter was detained by a store detective, police

A Girl in Blue

would be called to the store Manager's office to hear the facts.

'Officer, I saw this woman take a jumper from the display, put it in her carrier bag and leave the store without paying. When she was stopped she made no comment.'

Satisfied that an offence had been committed I would then caution the accused and make the arrest. The offenders could be anyone from middle-class women who blamed their out-of-character behaviour on Valium tablets, or elderly people who had fallen on hard times, or more often than not, the professional thief. I was once called to a popular department store where a gang of professional thieves were seen to fill an empty dustbin with ladies' clothing and run out without paying. Fortunately the theft had been observed by two male store detectives, who were able to overpower and detain the gang who were ultimately arrested and charged.

Another time I received a call to attend a store where a woman had been seen to take a leg of lamb from a freezer cabinet and put it up underneath her skirt then leave without paying. The woman was apprehended outside the store by the store detective, who called police to relate this chilling tale.

Most often, first-time offenders would plead guilty at the local magistrates' court. But now and again someone would proclaim their innocence and elect to be tried by judge and jury at the Crown Court, a court of criminal jurisdiction in Snaresbrook, north east London. The Court dealt with serious offences and those appeals that had been referred from the magistrates' court. Such referrals generally meant everyone concerned could wait around for hours before a case was eventually heard.

Hornchurch Manor

It was always possible that one's case wouldn't be heard the first day, especially if other cases on the court list took longer than expected. But once sworn in, the prosecution lawyer would ask for the police officer's evidence, then a likely cross-examination by the defence counsel would establish if one's compelling version of events was true. As far as the police were concerned the defender was definitely guilty, but the result depended on how effective the lawyers were and finally how the jury voted. First-time offenders would usually have to pay a fine, but very often defendants would re-offend only to go to court again, thereby risking a future custodial sentence.

Although I was stationed at the edge of the Metropolitan Police District, I was often called upon to work at demonstrations, escort marches or attend ceremonial events in central London. Women officers were always deployed as 'RT' - Radio transmission operators. So shortly after I arrived on Division I was sent on a one-day RT training course within Wandsworth Police Station. The room in which the course was held was right next door to where the Metropolitan police band practiced, not very conducive to sending or receiving messages. But enough was learnt in order to manage the equipment.

The demonstrations in central London we were sent on were considered to be tours of duty, most meant very early starts to enable police officers to be ready and in position along the designated route before it began. Women officers remained in the police transport coaches in side streets to man the radios; a woman's voice being deemed far clearer that that of a male officer in these circumstances.

Sometimes the day was uneventful, but on other occasions violence could suddenly erupt as it did when a group of demonstrators suddenly surged forward and

A Girl in Blue

surrounded the coach I was in. One person in the melee opened the coach door and threw a severed pig's head inside beside me. My reaction was to pick it up and to throw it right back into the crowd, lock the coach door and call on the radio for assistance.

During violent demonstrations officers were expected to face the mob with nothing more than blue serge, a helmet and a truncheon as protection, while being attacked with seriously effective weapons or missiles, or humiliatingly blasted with bags of white flour. Long before having riot training or being issued with protective gear police officers resorted to using dustbin lids as shields.

Demonstrations were not my favourite tour of duty, but police presence was necessary to keep law and order and to 'preserve public tranquility'.

A much more pleasant and memorable occasion in London was when I was on duty for the Trooping the Colour ceremony. I was told by the Inspector in charge of my unit to stand on the island beneath the Queen Victoria memorial in front of Buckingham Palace. I was standing in full uniform, wearing ceremonial duty white gloves, when Queen Elizabeth II rode past me on her horse en-route to Horse Guards Parade. As I stood respectfully to attention we looked at one another and a warm smile was exchanged. At such close quarters I noticed her appearance was much enhanced by heavy make-up, no doubt intentionally applied for the plethora of cameras that follow her every public move.

During such events refreshments for the police would be provided in huge marquees set up in St James' Park alongside the Mall. At breakfast, lunch or tea breaks, one would mingle with large numbers of both men and

Hornchurch Manor

women officers, all seconded from a variety of divisions throughout London. The experience of working on demos or ceremonials was exciting but nevertheless very tiring, as we could be standing for hours in all weathers come rain or shine until finally dismissed.

1971-72
Posted to Dagenham

After four years' service I was nudged over to Dagenham Police Station, KG.

Within Dagenham's labyrinth lies Becontree, a large housing estate approximately four square miles, which was completed in 1935 with around 100,000 working class residents moving into 26,000 new homes and what became the largest public housing estate in the world. The building of the estate hugely increased the population and led to demands on services. An additional 1,000 houses were added in later phases, as well as the May & Baker chemical factory and the Ford Motor plant.

I was one of two WPCs employed at KG, in Rainham Road South; again we were each on different shifts and were never short of work. I had unshackled myself from Crossy and was now under woman Sergeant Coey, although neither Teresa nor I saw her very much as her office was in East Ham nick. Also having a few years service under our belts we were considered to be able to get on with things on our own but if necessary we could seek advice at our police station from any male senior officer who happened to be vaguely interested in women police work.

I met a good many kitchen tables in Dagenham,

sometimes the only steady surface on which to write a statement. Once I was in a living room of a house where I had to interview a woman whose odour was so overpowering that, albeit reluctantly, I had to use the toilet where immediately I threw up. Nobody would have noticed any of my aftermath as the whole house smelt of sick anyway.

Cases which came my way involved domestic issues, missing people enquiries and road traffic incidents, and the shopping area at Dagenham Heathway always supplied police with the usual conveyor belt of shoplifters.

In any incident of sudden death, police are always informed. But sadly I was once called to a cot death at a council house near the Heathway, where I had the difficult job of comforting the parents. At that time I was not a mother but felt such sympathy, for a dead baby is a heart-wrenching sight, but as an investigator police had to be aware of the possible offence of infanticide, where the mother, by act or omission, causes the death of her less than twelve-month-old baby. In this particular incident the autopsy concluded that death was from natural causes, otherwise infanticide would have been punishable in the same way as manslaughter, although the decision would have depended on the opinion of the magistrate or jury.

At some point while living in Upminster, repairs to the hostel became necessary, so I was moved to Ede Section House in Mare Street, Hackney, east London. This establishment was far worse than Peto House or Upminster Hostel ever was. There was a male sergeant responsible for one hundred and thirty seven bedrooms, the well-being of the residents and good order of the premises. There were rules abound:

* All residents had to show consideration for others, be generally tidy and to treat the amenities with respect (residents being liable for any damage.)
* Bedrooms had to be kept tidy.
* Residents were advised to lock all personal belongings in the lockers or wardrobes provided.
* No furniture was to be put in bedrooms except those officially provided, unless by authority of the officer in charge.
* The method of attaching pictures etc to the walls was banned in case of damaging the fabric of the building.
* Gambling was prohibited.
* The use of the billiard table was permitted only between 10.30am and midnight (although in certain circumstances the District Commander might prohibit the use of the table before 12 noon. No explanation given as to why this was.)
* No electrical appliances were to be connected to the mains without the authority of the officer in charge.
* The use of radio and television sets was subject to the provisions of the Wireless Telegraphy Act 1949, and a valid licence would have to have been produced by each individual.
* Residents were not to adjust or interfere with the heating, electrical, mechanical, ventilating or other technical services.
* The cooking of food and preparation of hot drinks would be permitted only on officially provided equipment.
* Any residents who desired to sleep out had to inform their Chief Superintendent (or Detective

Chief Superintendent in the case of CID officers) of the address at which they would be staying.

Most of these restrictions now seem quite archaic, considering they were directed at responsible adults, but as we all know; rules are there to be broken. During the time I was living in the Ede Section House I was still suffering from being dumped by Charlie, so having to live in virtual solitary confinement in unfamiliar surroundings was difficult. However, another WPC who lived permanently at Ede House befriended me. She was an east Londoner, who everyone called 'Treasure'; not because she had a heart of gold, but because her colleagues wondered where on earth she had been dug up! Hardly a good example of a police officer, she was always unkempt with foul language to match. But having had a fair share of disastrous personal relationships herself, Treasure knew my pain and was for a while a perfect shoulder to cry on.

That is until I met Dan, a young PC who apart from being from a very well to do family was the owner of a Saab motor car. I made my interest in cars known to him so he was more than willing to take me out in it a few times. Then one thing led to another and I managed to get past the Section House Sergeant and into Dan's bed.

The relationship was short-lived as I only resided in Ede House for three weeks and during that time I still had to travel to and fro for duty in Dagenham, so when the call came to say that the renovations were complete I was relieved to return to live in virtually rule free Upminster.

I resided in the Upminster Hostel most of the time I worked in Essex. Several different housemates came and went, then not long after I left, the Hostel closed and what had been women police accommodation was returned to being Upminster police Station offices.

In 2012 the whole building, with all its history and memories was demolished to make way for a development of private houses, like has happened to so many other Met police stations over the years.

1972-73
Policing P Division

After a year working in Dagenham I decided to request a transfer to my favoured side of the Thames, to P Division whose divisional police station was in Lewisham. The posting was intended to allow me to be nearer my family home where I would be able to visit my parents more easily. My request was granted and in a matter of days I was posted as WPC 80P to Sydenham PS, a newly-built tower block consisting of the police station on the ground floor and living quarters on several upper floors to accommodate single male officers. Ironically, it was adjacent to the old decommissioned house where as a schoolgirl I had obtained the application form to join the Job. Seemingly, what goes around comes around!

Once again there were few women police officers on the division, so quite often I could be called upon to assist at other police stations such as Lewisham, Catford, Bromley or Penge. I chose not live at home for I was now twenty four, but instead moved into another women police hostel, this time in Canadian Avenue, Catford, a Victorian red-brick, double-fronted house close to the town centre. It had ten bedrooms, a communal kitchen and well appointed lounge. There were several bathrooms with cavernous baths and was far removed from the smaller four-bed semi in Upminster.

The premises housed about a dozen unmarried women officers and we all got on well, although like the women in the hostel in Upminster, due to different shifts the house was never full. I did get to know the first two policewomen who became drug-dog handlers, introduced in the early 1970s; their dogs lived outside the house in kennels in the manicured garden.

Since I had previously spent the majority of my teenage years in south London the area was more familiar and appealing than Essex, so finding my way around and understanding the public south of the river came far more naturally to me. Any blokes I came upon in the course of my work called me 'Babe', as well as everyone else, be they girlfriend, best friend, sister or boss. Sometimes even the dog got the 'Alright, Babe' treatment. And in due course I was to find out that the work of a woman police constable whichever side of the river remained much the same. There were the statements to be taken, missing people to trace and from time to time further demonstration duties in central London, crimes to solve and attendances at Court.

Each week when Deptford Juvenile Court sat I acted as Matron, the impartial support for attendees, checking court lists and explaining any necessary court procedures to the uninitiated.

A Juvenile Court, or Youth Court as it was later referred to, was less formal than an adult court and members of the public were not allowed into the court without permission, and young people were called by their first name. Typical offences for which children or young people had to appear before the court, were theft and burglary, anti-social behaviour and drugs offences.

For serious crimes such as murder or rape, cases started in the youth court and were then referred to a Crown Court.

From time to time, I worked with a colleague, Station Sergeant Glynn Evans, who everyone called Taffy. One day he asked me to assist him with a job in Lower Sydenham.

On arrival at our destination Taffy parked our car a little way away from the targeted site. Sydenham Road was as busy as usual at midday on a Friday, so the presence of a blue Panda car would not create too much interest. For a few minutes Taffy and I sat in the car while he explained further.

'Police have received reports from several members of the public that indecent acts have been taking place in the men's public toilet.'

'I presume the toilets over there?'

'Yes, they're the only ones used by the public in Lower Sydenham.'

Then, just as Taffy was talking, we saw two men walk into the men's toilet. After some ten minutes, longer than most people take to do their business in a public convenience, neither had appeared from within. So Taffy said, 'Let's go!'

We jumped out of the police car and ran across the road.

'I'm going in, you cover the exit door.'

Seconds after Taffy disappeared inside the toilet a male of about fifty years of age ran straight out and into my arms with a thud almost knocking me off my feet, but I hung on to him tightly. Being nabbed by a woman police officer always seemed to be more of a shock to an offender than being arrested at all. Within seconds Taffy came out with the other man who was struggling and shouting his innocence, but due to my sergeant witnessing the two men committing an act of gross indecency in a public place, both men were arrested under the Sexual Offences Act 1967.

Taffy called up for assistance and another Panda car arrived so that the men could be taken separately to Sydenham police station to be charged, neither kept in custody but bailed to await further details about when they would appear at Court. Back at the nick, Taffy's complimented me by saying, 'Good work kid.' I only did what I instinctively had to do.

In the early seventies Rolf Harris, the now-disgraced entertainer, lived on Sydenham's ground. At one time he was involved in a traffic incident, but because he did not have his documents with him he was given a form by a police officer, known as a HORT 1. The driver recorded details of the vehicle, the name, address, date of birth of the driver/owner and would then take the completed form, together with their insurance and driving licence, to a police station of their choice. But due to his celebrity status, the station sergeant at Sydenham police station decided that instead of Mr Harris having to attend the station within the required seven days, police would visit him at his home address. So I and a male colleague were quite excited about being assigned to the job for we both recalled how as children we had seen Rolf creating cartoon drawings on a children's TV show called *Jigsaw*, and also on *Whirligig*, which featured a character called 'Willoughby' who sprang to life on a drawing board. And of course we recalled the memorable recordings of *Two Little Boys* and *Tie Me Kangaroo Down*.

When we arrived at Rolf Harris's house we saw that he was living in two obviously sixties-designed houses

Policing P Division

linked together as one. The interior was a fascinating assemblage of his own and his wife's artworks and astonishingly they had a native Australian eucalyptus tree growing inside the house.

Rolf was less of an entertainer than I expected, so I did not dare to mention the fond childhood memories I had of him. Consequently my colleague and I got on with the business we had gone to see him for, satisfactorily checked his driving documents and left.

The usual round of enquiries continued, but an interesting investigation with which I was involved happened at a dry cleaners in Catford. Customers deposited articles they wanted cleaned, but when they arrived to collect several customers were informed that their clothes had gone missing or somehow there was a problem with their cleaning ticket. Subsequently it was discovered that the clothes which had gone missing were designer-label and were being sold on by the owners of the dry cleaners, who were subsequently arrested and charged with theft.

I really enjoyed driving on duty, except on the occasions that I had to drive Sydenham station's Austin LD van, a smaller version of a Black Maria, but no-one had ever prepared me to drive such a large vehicle that also had an unwieldy, stiff column gear change. The LD van was launched in 1954 and discontinued in 1967, so by 1970 after continual use it was definitely showing signs of wear. Furthermore, the LD was totally unsuited to my physique as my legs only just about reached the pedals; how I managed to avoid accidents or control the monster on hill-starts beggar's belief! Although when no other vehicles were available at the station, I did drive it to various enquiries around the streets of south east London.

A Girl in Blue

Whilst I was Sydenham police station I had a three-month tour of duty attached to Scotland Yard's B11 Department, the prison van service, not as a driver but as an escort on the women's prison van, working out of a large pound at the south west foot of Vauxhall Bridge. I would journey there in my Hillman Imp and park alongside rows of green buses, known as Green Goddesses that served the whole of the Metropolitan Police District. On my first day it was a relief to be met by my driver PC Milne, who I had worked with previously at Romford. He kindly helped me by explaining the daily ritual:

'First thing to do is go and have a cup of tea.'

I had come to think by now that the police force was founded on tea!

'Then what?'

'Get the list from the office. Every day we must leave the garage at 7am to get to various police stations in south east London to pick up females who have been arrested, mainly drunks or Toms, and kept in custody overnight.'

'Then we take them to Court.'

'Yep.'

At each police station I would be met by the custody sergeant as was the case when I arrived at Southwark for my first encounter with a prison van passenger.

'Morning love, this is Molly, NFA,' handing over an unkempt woman to me who I tried to keep at a satisfactory distance due to the pungent alcoholic fumes she was breathing over everyone. 'Molly,' I said, 'Be a good girl and get in the van.'

'Piss off copper!' she shouted in my ear as she staggered to the door of van and struggled to be free of my hold. Fortunately the effects of her previous night's drinking had hardly worn off so there was little strength in her protestations, but sober or not to Court she was duly taken. Being of no fixed abode Molly was dealt with by a Magistrate, and depending on her previous convictions there was every possibility she was sent to live in one of London's women's refuges. Adrian, PC Milne and I never saw that particular woman again, although we encountered all sorts. For some unknown reason I seemed to attract transvestites, especially those whose five o'clock shadow was clearly evident by the early hours of the morning. It was a good tour, full of variety and surprises.

The Metropolitan Police District grew to 1,578 square kilometres in 1975, with twenty four divisions stretching from north to south, east to west. At some time during my service for one reason or another I had contact with most of them, either by being required to work there, to liaise with officers at other police stations, or when work necessitated the transfer of a female prisoner.

Members of the public are generally only aware of the area of London in which they were born or raised or maybe their workplace district but the knowledge I gained of London and its communities was invaluable.

On 11th June 1972 I was off duty in Catford when the Divisional Station Inspector rang me late into the night explaining that at approximately 9.30 p.m. there had been a train crash in Eltham and as many police officers as possible were needed at the scene.

I responded immediately to his order, and sometime after midnight I arrived and parked my car as close as possible to where the crash had happened. It was a scene of utter mayhem, sights nightmares are made of with five or six crumpled train carriages cast down the embankment. Several ambulances had already arrived and the flashing blue lights of police cars punctuated the darkness. From amongst the eerie scene came shouts of help. A police officer in uniform approached me ready to prevent access, but when I showed him my warrant card he said:

'It's a pretty horrible sight, but we need as much help as we can get.'

'What's best to do?' I asked.

'The ambulance crews are dealing with the worst victims, the fire brigade are working to release casualties from the wreckage, so best you deal with the walking wounded.'

With that a woman came staggering toward me, her face covered with blood. My First Aid training was invaluable, as not only was the woman's face injured but she had lost part of her left arm below the elbow. She was screaming in pain. I informed her who I was and she managed to cry out, 'Mabel, I'm Mabel.' She was very weak and I thought she would collapse, but while offering her as much comfort as possible I got her onto the grass and utilised the belt of her skirt as a temporary tourniquet. One of the ambulance crew intervened and they transported her to the nearby hospital along with some of the other injured victims. All the emergency services worked tirelessly through the night and into the next day. I stayed comforting and assisting with the injured until there was nothing more I could do for exhaustion overcame me.

In time I learned that the train was the diesel-hauled five past eight Margate to Kentish Town excursion train. It comprised of ten coaches, filled with passengers returning from a day's outing to the coast. The driver had failed to take any braking action to reduce his train's speed on the steeply-falling gradient through Eltham Park to Eltham (Well Hall) in preparation for entering the right-hand curve just beyond Well Hall station. The cause of the driver's failure was that he had grossly impaired his ability to drive safely by drinking a considerable quantity of alcohol both before and after booking on duty. Five passengers in the train and its driver lost their lives, and one hundred and twenty six people including the second man on the locomotive were injured. Forty of those taken to hospital were detained, some of them being very seriously injured. The original death toll among the passengers was three, but one died of his injuries in November and another of her injuries in mid-August. I hoped that it was not Mabel.

On a more pleasant topic, also in the summer of 1972 I found out that the American singer Andy Williams was to perform at the Crystal Palace Bowl, just outside Sydenham's ground. It was to be the first venue of his European tour and as my friend Marilyn was an avid fan, she pleaded with me to try to get her a ticket. So I decided to go one better and get her into the event with me. When the day of his appearance dawned she, and I in plain clothes, entered the park. We side-stepped the queue and I approached one of the security men at the gate.

'This lady and I need to come into the event.'

We were both young-looking twenty four year olds, so security was somewhat taken aback when I showed him my warrant card. I had pre-warned Marilyn to 'remain silent', for on this occasion it would be me doing all the talking. On seeing my ID, Marilyn and I were allowed to enter and once inside sat ourselves amongst an audience of some ten thousand people on the grassy bank beside the lake on a beautiful August evening under a forget-me-not sky.

Although it was my day off, a police officer is on duty 24/7 so had there been something for me to deal with I would not have been able to ignore it. Fortunately, nothing untoward did occur so listening to the harmonious tones of one of the world's greatest stars was utterly memorable, and the fact that neither of us had to pay the £2 entrance fee made it even more so.

While living in the Catford Hostel there were a few romances. One of my friends married a solicitor but afterwards she resigned from the police and the couple went to live in Surrey. Another very good police officer, Mary, pined for her native Cornwall, so after a career of about four years she too resigned and returned home.

Another WPC eloped by car to Torquay with a stylish temporary detective constable (who would have made a good double for David Essex). She had met him through work on a robbery case and, after only a few weeks, she and the TDC ended up in Torquay absent without leave. Telling no-one - not their families nor their regular partners - about what they intended to do, or where they were, they managed to get married but on their return to work about a week later both were formally reprimanded by their superiors. They tried to get the marriage annulled because from the start they realised it had all been a huge mistake, but each had to wait two years for a divorce. In the meantime, the TDC was served with a disciplinary form (a '163') and was asked to leave the force, whereas under a cloud of disappointment the WPC decided to resign. Women police careers tended to be short back in the day, some only joining to nab themselves a husband, but in time many did go up the ranks, married or not.

Policing P Division

In the latter stages of my career in south London I continued to enjoy my work on division carrying out the usual enquiries, and from time-to-time assisted male officers with various investigations. However, my work developed to giving talks about police work to women's groups such as the Women's Institute, and I also visited many primary schools to inform young pupils about strangers and how to say 'No' to such perpetrators along with a 'Stranger Danger!' slogan.

Being in close proximity to children sparked an idea within me that a career in teaching might be possible at sometime in the future, but having no teaching qualification or a degree in education, the idea was temporarily shelved.

By the time I got to Sydenham Police Station I was seriously dating James, whom I had met at a mutual friend's engagement party at police-married quarters in Paddington a year or so earlier. As an 18-year-old Cadet he had initially been posted to Greenwich Police Station, where I later discovered that, during a period of separation from one another, he had had a brief encounter with Muriel the serial bride, but apparently all he ever spoke about was me. So she was not at all surprised to hear that we had finally got together.

Some years after leaving the police I was pleased to receive a letter from her:

> Dear Lo,
>
> My first marriage was to a police officer from M Division, but this lasted approximately six months. The second was to another policeman, with whom I was deeply in love. I expected the match would last forever, but just as we were about to be offered a little boy for adoption, my heart was broken when I discovered that

A Girl in Blue

my husband had been having an affair with a hairdresser. During one of my many trips overseas I met and married an American. Then I went on to study nursing and I am enjoying life in California with husband number three.

Mu

Muriel would have suited America, and America would have suited her but her life in the Met was a prime example of short lived relationships. Sometimes due to the pressure of work, or the temptations that could often be put in one's way.

As for James, after his time as a cadet in Greenwich and thereafter his initial training at Hendon, he was posted to Holloway Police Station. By then I was living in the hostel in Catford, some considerable distance from his Section House in Caledonian Road, north London, but absence did make our hearts grow fonder and in 1975 I became a policeman's wife.

Daphne transferred to Tottenham police station, and she and her husband continued to be our lifelong friends. Carol's marriage, to a policeman who rose to the rank of uniform Inspector ended in divorce, while she went on to be a Detective Sergeant, eventually retiring on ill health some twenty years after joining. In later years I phoned her to ask her personal recollections of our time together in Romford, and she was able to reinforce much of what I have documented here. Whilst speaking to her it was clearly evident that having worked so long in London her accent had changed and I could understand her every word!

Tish married a Metropolitan PC she met on a blind date and they transferred to the Kent Constabulary, and I discovered through a mutual friend that Pat H had married an Australian farmer, who took her back to his homeland where she joined the New South Wales police force.

When I was married and with children of my own I only saw my natural father once more, after we were reluctantly invited by his wife to their home in Weymouth as he was nearing the end of his life. My mother lived until she was 85. Of course she mellowed as she got older, and towards the end our relationship was good and I was more able to appreciate all the meaningful things she had done for me. We had gone through good times and bad together, but without those experiences I would not have become the independent, capable adult of whom she was so proud. Douglas too had been a great influence, imparting much of his characteristic stiff upper lip approach to life on me. He lived until he was 102.

1973
'Times They are a Changing'

And so it was in 1973 that the work of the WPC began to change. Woman Commander Shirley Becke was of the opinion that women police officers' specialties had become restrictive, so she and the Commissioner, Sir Robert Mark, who had taken up office in 1972, decided integration was the only solution. This idea had been discussed for some time prior to 1973, but two years before the Sex Discrimination Act was passed the Metropolitan women police branch ceased to exist, along with what had been the very effective A4 branch at New Scotland Yard, and integration came about.

'What use is she going to be? Her place is at home beside the kitchen sink!' summed up some male officers' attitudes to integration, being convinced that women would be unable to work alongside them as equals and would further question whether women officers would be mentally as well as physically tough enough to stand alongside them. They in fact had short memories for women police were always willing to work with male colleagues but this drastic change of working conditions brought an end to the careers of more than a few women police officers. Even the lure of equal pay could not entice them to stay, myself included. I could see that women banging the drum for equality at the time were going too far, and in many respects have lived to regret it.

As the anthropologist Dame Mary Douglas said:

> Real equality is immensely difficult to achieve. It needs continual revision and monitoring of distributions. And it does not provide buffers between members so they are continually colliding or frustrating each other.

So it was with a heavy heart that I returned my uniform, my appointments and my warrant card to my superior officer.

1973
End of an Era

While serving as a woman police constable I experienced life in all its different guises but most of all it was a privilege to serve Queen and country and to uphold the values set by Sir Richard Mayne in 1829. I had five-and-half years of the best of times. I was fortunate to have worked in the east, the west and the south of London, a rare experience for any officer. There were moments when things didn't quite go to plan, especially in my private life, but thankfully I emerged unscathed, unlike those courageous police officers both in and out of uniform who did die in the line of duty.

Nobody sees more of human life in a career than a police officer, and the old adage 'Once a copper always a copper' applies today as much as it ever did.

In the aftermath of integration, WPCs lost their unique appendage and became PCs, equal to their colleagues in all but gender. Many women disapproved of equality, but protocol and political correctness dictated the 'W' was dropped and change happened.

Today, women in the police service continue to increase in number and are going from strength to strength, many reaching senior ranks and now for the first time in its one hundred and ninety year history, a woman, Cressida

Dick has been appointed as the Commissioner of the Metropolis.

So if anyone asks me what it was like serving as a woman officer in the greatest police service in the world, my answer can only be that it was definitely an incredible rite of passage for a particularly naïve nineteen-year-old; and the memories I have of that time and throughout my service will remain with me forever, as it would for many other ex women officers.

It is said that one can make friends for a season, some for a reason and some for life and that is certainly what happened to me. I met so many interesting and memorable people, some I would never have had the pleasure of meeting had it not been for my time in the police.

Recently I went the funeral of a former male colleague who like many of the other mourners had joined the Job in the 1960s. The occasion was well attended and at the wake following the service we group of ex officers reminisced about our time in the Force. Stories were exchanged about the camaraderie we enjoyed in times gone by, and of the oft-difficult jobs with which all of us at one time or another had to deal. And those colleagues who had worked closely with the deceased also recalled some of the amusing incidents in which he was involved during his 30-year career. Pranks that today would be totally non-politically correct and would undoubtedly end a police officer's employ.

Then just before we were all about to go our separate ways, one of the retired policemen who I knew had risen to the rank of Chief Superintendent stopped, looked at me - the only woman in the group - and made a profound remark.

'I must take this opportunity to tell you that prior to integration in 1973, WPCs with whom we worked were revered by both male officers and the public. In fact, they were looked up to in awe and I applaud you for the work you did.'

The others in the group nodded with approval, and I too knew exactly what he meant.

Index

A4 Branch (Women Police), New Scotland Yard, 42, 62; index of juveniles, 84, 86, 129; disbanded, 197
A127 (Southend Arterial Road), 131–2, 133–5, 136
ABC cinema, Cheltenham, 26
abortion, 3, 68
Acton, WPC Daphne, 112, 113–15, 121, 194
Agnes, Sister (of St Gregory's school), 12
Aliens Enquiries, 169–70
Alpine coffee bar, Forest Hill, 37
animals on the road, 133–5
Anita (approved school absconder), 117
appointments (equipment and accessories), 61–2, 81, 113
Arden, Elizabeth, 90
armlets, 58
Austin Cambridge (car), 40
Austin-Healey Sprite (car), 65
Austin LD van, 187

B11 (prison van service), New Scotland Yard, 188–9
Babes in the Wood murders (1970), 114
Bacon, Francis, 162
Bailey, WPC Mary, 51, 77
Barking Police Station hostel, 88
Bather, Chief Superintendent Elizabeth, 62
'Bather' uniform, 62, 112–13

beat patrols, 90, 93, 154–5
Becke, Chief Superintendent Shirley, 42–4, 75, 197
Becontree housing estate, Dagenham, 177
Belcher, Muriel, 161
Ben (gardener), 9
Bermondsey, 17, 18–22, 23–4, 29, 36, 42
Bernadette, Sister (of St Gregory's school), 11–14
Beryl (WPC at Romford), 87–8, 112
Betty and Beatie (Bermondsey twins), 19
Bexley, Kent, 29, 68
Blackheath Common, 38
Blewitt, Sergeant (Peel House drill officer), 59
Blyton, Enid, 10
body cameras, 122
Brain Committee (Interdepartmental Committee on Drug Addiction), 107
Bramcote Arms, Bermondsey, 18
breathalyser tests, 132–3
Bridget (police matron), 145
Brignall, Douglas (Gert's common-law husband): background, 29; Gert and Lois move in with, 29–30; and Lois's upbringing, 30, 31–2, 47, 65, 151; drives Lois to police job interview, 40;

203

Index

gives celebration lunch for Lois, 75; death, 195
British Board of Film Censors, 25
Bromley Court Hotel (music venue), 35
brothels, 157–8, 165–6
Brownies (Girl Guides), 16
Buckingham Palace, 55, 174

cannabis: campaign to legalise (1967), 107; 'Pot Party' raid, 109–10; Sue (cannabis plant grower), 89
capes, 112–13
care and protection work, 84–6, 116–17, 127–9, 130, 137–40, 144–6, 148–9, 168–9
careless driving, 131–2
Carol *see* Hood, WPC Carol
Castle, Barbara, 137
Catford, 187
Catford police hostel, 183–4, 192, 194
Charlie (Lois's boyfriend), 141–2, 167, 180
Charlie (police officer at West Ham), 96–7
Chas (Charlie's father), 142
Cheltenham, 5, 9, 10, 25–6; *see also* Royston; St Gregory's primary school
Cheltenham General Hospital, 14–15
Cheltenham Races, 9
Children and Young Persons Act 1933, 68
Chinese gaming clubs (Soho), 160–1
CID (Criminal Investigation Department): drugs raids, 169; female officers, 170; Gidea Park abandoned baby case, 104–5; handling and questioning of suspects, 105–6; and Harold Hill suicide case, 149; partying, 140; 'Q' cars, 83; Romford off-licence robbery, 94–5 cinema, 25–6
Clark, Bill (Lois's father): meets and sets up home with Gert, 3–4; birth of daughter Lois, 4; appearance, 6; business ventures, 6, 10; relations with Lois, 8, 9–10; family trip through Europe, 16–17; Gert and Lois leave, 17; phone calls from Lois, 22, 25–6; engagement to Gert, 26; sued for Breach of Promise, 27; later life, 195
Clark, Emily Jane (Lois's grandmother), 5–6
Clubs Office *see* Vice Squad
Coey, Sergeant (at East Ham Police Station), 177
collar numbers, 81, 96, 97–8
Collingwood Secondary School, New Cross, 30
Colony Room (Soho drinking club), 161–2
common assault, definition, 59–60
constables, parish, 39
Cornelius (hippy), 108
Coronation (1953), 15–16
cot death, 178
court procedure training, 70–2
court referral system, 172
Criminal Investigation Department *see* CID
Crispin Villa, Cheltenham, 10
Criterion ice cream parlour, Sydenham, 38
Cross, Sergeant Edith ('Crossy'): at Romford Police Station, 80, 82, 84, 90, 99, 147; described, 90; reports Lois, 123; visits Upminster Police Station, 125
crowd control, 173–4
Crystal Palace, destroyed by fire,

Index

22
Crystal Palace Bowl (concert venue), 191–2
Cudham, Kent, 31
custody of women and young persons, 97, 112
cycling offences, 147

Dagenham, 103–4, 177–8; Becontree housing estate, 177; Ford sewing machinists' strike (1968), 136–7
Dagenham Police Station, 177
Dan (police officer), 180
dangerous dogs, 168
Dangerous Drugs Act 1965, 107
Daphne *see* Acton, WPC Daphne
Dean Street, Soho, 159, 161
death notices, 114–15
decoy operations, 170–1
demonstrations and ceremonial events, 173–5
Deptford Juvenile Court, 184
Dick, Cressida (Commissioner of Metropolitan Police 2017–present), 199–200
dogs: dangerous, 168; drug dogs, 184
domestic disputes, 93, 147
Doreen (police officer), 82–3, 84–6
Dossetor, Ernest, 146
Douglas, Dame Mary, 198
drill practice, 58–9
drink driving offences, 132–3
drug dogs, 184
drugs, illegal, 107, 109–10, 169
drunk and disorderly offences, 91–2, 93, 130
drunk in charge of a child, 93, 130

Easter, James (Lois's husband), 193, 194
Ede Section House, Hackney, 178–80
Elizabeth II, Queen, 16, 174
Eltham Well Hall rail crash (1972), 189–91
England, PC Leslie, 97
Essex Constabulary, 80, 81, 89, 120
Evans, Sergeant Glynn ('Taffy'), 185–6
Evans, WPC (at Walworth Police Station), 73–4
evidence-giving in court, 70–2

film censorship, 25
fingerprinting, 56, 97
First Aid and lifesaving training, 68–9
Flower Children, 107–10, 137
Ford sewing machinists' strike (1968), 136–7
Fry, Elizabeth, 39

gaming clubs, 157, 160–1
Gargoyle Club, Soho, 159–60
Garland, Julie, 13
Gerrard Street, Soho, 160–1
Gidea Park, 146–7, 155; abandoned baby case, 104–5; Raphael Park 'love-in' (1967), 107–9
Girl Guides, 16, 31
Glenlyn Ballroom (club), Forest Hill, 34–5
Green, Johnny, 14
Gunmaker (public house), Marylebone, 65

handover and message books, 82, 115, 116–17
Harold Hill council estate, 89, 142–3, 143n, 148–9
Harris, Rolf, 186–7
Harrow Lodge park, Hornchurch, 171
Harry (police officer), 133–5
Hartnell, William, 43–4, 112–13

205

Index

hats, 72, 112
'Heather' (Soho prostitute), 163–5
Hendon Police Training School, 56, 69; driving school, 151–4
Henry (CID officer), 104–5
Hillman Imp (car), 155–6, 187
Hindley, Myra, plans escape from Holloway, 143–4
hippies *see* Flower Children
Holloway Prison, 73, 143–4
Hood, WPC Carol: meets Lois at interview, 40–1; shares room with Lois at Peto House, 51; warns of lecherous instructor, 69; posted to Romford, 76–7, 79–81; boyfriend Ken, 77; at Upminster police hostel, 87–8; loses contact with Lois, 111; later life, 194
Hornchurch: Harrow Lodge park, 171; St Leonard's Children's Home, 168–9
Hornchurch Police Station, 167
hostels *see* Barking Police Station hostel; Catford police hostel; Pembridge Hall; Upminster police hostel
Household Cavalry, 55
Hunt, Frederick Robert (Lois's grandfather), 17–18
Hunt, Gertrude (*née* Neal; Lois's grandmother), 17–18, 20
Hutchins, Sergeant Frederick: murdered in line of duty, 96–8

Ibiza, 137
Ilderton Road primary school, Bermondsey, 19, 30
Ilford Palais raid (1971), 169
immigration, 91, 169–70
indecent exposure, 171
infanticide, 178
initiation ceremonies, 98–9, 121

Instruction Book (for constables), 57–8
interview methods of CID, 105–6
Ivy (Lewisham catering manager), 33

Jack (police officer), 132–3
Jeff (Vice Squad officer), 159–60, 161–2
'Jenny' (career offender), 142–4
Joe's ice cream parlour, Bermondsey, 21
Jones, Detective Inspector George, 96
Juvenile Courts, 116, 139–40, 144–5, 184–5

Ken (Carol Hood's boyfriend), 77
King, Sergeant Sylvia, 57
knickers, 113

Leblanc, Madame (school teacher), 30
Lewisham, 33–4
lifesaving training, 69
Linda (police recruit), 51–2, 77–8
littering, 147
London General Hospital, Denmark Hill, 18
Lownes, Victor, 161

Mabel (train crash victim), 190, 191
marijuana *see* cannabis
Marilyn (Lois's lifelong friend), 30–1, 137, 191–2
Mark, Sir Robert (Commissioner of Metropolitan Police 1972–77), 197
Mary (police officer), 192
matrons: in Juvenile Courts, 145, 184; in women's prisons, 39

Index

Mavis (cook at Peto House), 52
Mayfair brothel, 165–6
Mayne, Sir Richard, 57–8, 199
McNab, Sergeant (Warden at Peto House), 49–50, 51, 52, 64
Melvyn (teenage crush), 38
mental health patients, 129–30
message books, 82, 115, 116–17
Metropolitan Police: area, 80, 189; cadets, 113; Commissioners, 136, 197, 199–200; officers murdered on duty, 36–7, 96–8; primary objectives, 57–8; *see also* CID; Hendon Police College; New Scotland Yard; Peel House; women police; and names of individual officers and stations
Metropolitan Police Act 1839, 93
Middleton, Mr (Cheltenham solicitor), 16
Miles, Inspector Honor, 147–8, 151
milk lorry spillage, 136
Milne, PC Adrian, 188–9
missing person enquiries, 84–6, 102–3, 115–20, 127–9
Molly (Southwark prisoner), 188–9
Morgan, Inspector (at Harold Hill Police Station), 89
Mott, Mr (Sydenham pharmacist), 34
Mountain Ash, Cynon Valley, 139–40
Muriel ('Mu'; police officer): at Peto House, 51–2; at Pembridge Hall, 75; appearance and background, 77; posted to Shooter's Hill Police Station, 77; career in R Division, 78; relationship with James Easter, 193; later life, 193–4

Nelly (vagrant), 74
New Scotland Yard: A4 Branch (women police), 42, 62, 84, 86, 129, 197; B11 Branch (prison van service), 188–9; Daphne Acton works for, 113; Fingerprint Branch, 56; information operations room, 103–4; Lois summoned to, 123–5; new recruit formalities, 75; Panda cars, 154; Police Orders, 82
Newport House (remand home), Great Baddow, 145–6
night duty, 90–3
'Nuclear Ned' (First Aid instructor), 69

oath of allegiance, 56
obscene publications industry, 157
O'Donoghue, Dee, 130
'Old Bill': origin of term, 101
Oldchurch Hospital mortuary, 98
Orchid Ballroom, Purley, 35

PACE (Police and Criminal Evidence Act 1984), 106
Panda cars, 131, 154–5
parish constables, 39
Pat H (police officer), 115, 123, 125, 194–5
Pat (police officer) *see* Tish
patrolling, 90, 93, 154–5
Pawsey, Inspector Philip: murdered in line of duty, 97
Pedoscope, 13 & n
Peel, Sir Robert, 55, 76
Peel House (Metropolitan Police training school), 55–64, 65–73; accommodation, 56, 73; end of course dance, 75
Pembridge Hall, Bayswater, 72, 75

207

Index

Peto, Superintendent Dorothy, 47
Peto House (Metropolitan Police Section House), 47, 49–53, 61, 64, 72, 73
pickpockets, 99–102
pirate radio stations, 52n
Playboy Club, Soho, 161
'Plonk', use of term, 120
pocket notebooks, 62, 113, 147
Police and Criminal Evidence Act 1984 (PACE), 106
Police Boxes, 103–4, 103n
Police Cadets, 113
Police Orders, 82, 113, 122
policewomen *see* women police
pop music, 35–6, 127–8
prison matrons, 39
prison van service (B11), 188–9
prisoner escort duties, 188–9
prostitutes/prostitution, 157, 163–6
public footbaths, 20–1

questioning of suspects, 105–6

Rachel (missing person case), 127–9
Radio London, 52n
radio transmission (RT) operators, 173–4
Rainham Police Station, 89
rape, 68, 144, 170
Raphael Park, Romford: 'love-in' (1967), 107–9
remand homes, 145–6
rent aid, 87
Representation of the People Act 1928, 24
riding on the pavement, 147
Rita (police officer), 112
road policing, 130–6
Road Safety Act 1967, 132
road traffic accidents, 66, 135–6, 153
Roadcraft (car control system), 151, 152
Romford: coal yard, 85–6; market, 93–4, 99–102; night life, 91–2; Odeon cinema, 127–9; off-licence robbery, 94–5; police sub-division, 88–9; *see also* Gidea Park
Romford Juvenile Court, 139
Romford Magistrates' Court, 80, 92, 102
Romford Police Station, 79–81, 82–3, 91, 92
Ronnie Scott's Jazz Club, 163
Royston (*later* Royston Hotel), Cheltenham, 5 & n, 6–9, 26–7
Rube (police recruit at Peel House), 62–3
Russell, PC (Rusty), 99–102

St Francis' primary school, Peckham, 30
St Gregory's primary school, Cheltenham, 11–14, 15
St Leonard's Children's Home, Hornchurch, 168–9
Salter, Sergeant (in Mountain Ash), 139
saluting, 63–4
school-crossing patrols, 167–8
Scotland Yard *see* New Scotland Yard
Scrivens, Miss (remand home matron), 146
seat belt legislation, 153
section houses *see* Ede Section House; Peto House
self-defence and physical restraint training, 69
Serpentine Restaurant, Hyde Park, 75
Sex Discrimination Act 1975, 197
sexual harassment and intimidation, 57, 67, 69, 98, 120–2
sexual offences, 68, 144, 165,

Index

170–1, 185–6
Sexual Offences Act 1956, 165
Sexual Offences Act 1967, 186
Shepherd, Graham, 65, 75, 77, 123–5, 141
Shepherd's Bush murders (1966), 36–7
shoeshining, 62–3
shoplifting, 171–3
Simpson, Sir Joseph (Commissioner of Metropolitan Police 1958–68), 136
Skillicorne, Captain Henry, 5n
Skillicorne, William Nash, 5n
Snaresbrook Crown Court, 172–3
Soho, 155–6, 157, 159–63
Southwark Crown Court, 72
Southwark Police Station, 188
Standard Flying 8 (car), 9–10
Stanley, Superintendent Sofia, 122
statement taking, 68, 170
Steampacket (blues band), 35
Stella (police officer), 119–20
Stoke Newington drugs raid (1971), 169
stop and search powers, 93, 107
store detectives, 171–2
Street Offences Act 1959, 68, 157, 163
Sue (cannabis plant grower), 89
Suffragette movement, 24, 90
suicides, 148–9
'Summer of Love' (1967), 107–10
Summers, John (Lois's brother-in-law), 36, 37, 42–3, 166
Sunday Express, 97
Surrey Docks, London: bombed during war, 24
'Surrey' uniform, 113
Sweet, Miss (music teacher), 22
swimming instruction, 69–70
switchboard operators, 140–1

Sydenham, 29–30, 34, 38, 185–7
Sydenham Girls School, 30–2, 33
Sydenham Police Station, 37, 183, 186

'Taffy' *see* Evans, Sergeant Glynn
Taylor, Superintendent Win, 123–5
tea making duties, 120
television, 15–16
Teresa (police officer at Dagenham), 177
Thomas, Bronwyn, 137–40
'Tish' *see* Pat
Tobias family (of Romford), 94–5
Tony (police officer), 83–4
Tower Bridge Magistrates' Court, 27
'Tracy' (juvenile), 144
traffic policing, 130–6
'Treasure' (police officer at Hackney), 180
Trevor (police officer), 131–2
Trooping the Colour (1971), 174
truncheons, 61–2, 113
Tweedie, Fred, 84–6
Twiggy (Sixties model), 142

underage sex, 144
uniform inspection, 62–3
uniforms, women police, 43–4, 58, 61, 62, 108, 112–13
Uniquip (clothing manufacturer), 61
Upminster: dog attack incident, 168; 'Pot Party' raid, 109–10; railway station, 130
Upminster police hostel, 87–8, 92, 111–12, 114, 122–5, 140, 178; closed and demolished, 180–1
Upminster Police Station, 87,

Index

109, 168

vagrancy, 74
Vaughn, Detective Constable Ray, 117–20
Vaughn, Yvonne, 117–20
Verney Road (No 123), Bermondsey, 17, 18, 20, 21–2
Vice Squad, 43, 157–66; selection process, 162
Vivienne (Charlie's mother), 142

Waldron, Sir John (Commissioner of Metropolitan Police 1968-72), 136
Wall, Superintendent Tommy, 66–8, 76
Walworth Road Police Station, 73–4
Wandsworth Police Station, 173
Warley Mental Hospital, Essex, 129
warrant cards, 75
Watchmen, 39
West End Central Police Station, 157, 158–9, 166
West Ham police murders (1961), 96–8
West Ham Police Station, 96
whistles and chains, 81, 113
White Swan (public house), Victoria, 65
Williams, Andy: concert (1972), 191–2
Williams, Linda, 137–40
Willoughby, Alf, 3, 4
Willoughby, Brenda (*later* Summers; Lois's half-sister), 3, 9, 29, 36, 68
Willoughby, Gertrude 'Gert' (*née* Hunt; Lois's mother): childhood in Bermondsey, 23–4; studies Domestic Science, 6; watches Crystal Palace fire (1936), 22; marriage to Alf Willoughby and birth of children, 3; terminates unwanted pregnancy, 3, 68; deserts family, 3–4; second family with Bill Clark, 4; names Lois, 5; takes Lois to see dying grandfather, 18; household and domestic chores, 6, 7–8, 10; family life, 9–10, 13, 15–16; trip through Europe (1955), 16–17; leaves Bill and moves to Bermondsey with Lois, 17, 24; relations with Lois, 20–1, 22–3, 26; engagement to Bill, 26; jilted and wins damages for Breach of Promise, 27; bank cashier at Peckham, 29; meets and sets up home with Douglas Brignall, 29–30; and Lois's future career, 32; showdowns with Lois, 32, 36, 38; Lois leaves home, 47; leaving presents to Lois, 52–3, 111; shops with Lois in West End, 72; gives celebration lunch for Lois, 75; later life and death, 195
Willoughby, Ralph (Lois's half-brother), 3, 7, 9
WILLOUGHBY-EASTER, LOIS (*née* Willoughby):
Early life: family background, 3–4; birth, 4; naming, 5; taken to see dying grandfather, 18; early childhood in Cheltenham, 6–16; appearance, 6; writes to Enid Blyton, 10; at primary school, 11–14, 15; tonsils removed, 14–15; piano lessons, 22; in the Brownies, 16; love of cinema, 25–6; family trip through Europe (1955), 16–17; moves to Bermondsey

Index

with mother, 17; childhood in Bermondsey, 19–26; at junior school, 19; name change, 20; relationship with mother, 20–1, 22–3; continued contact with father, 22, 25–6; briefly returns to live with father, 26–7; back in Bermondsey, 29; hit by speeding car, 42; settles in Sydenham with mother and Douglas, 29–30; at Sydenham Girls School, 30–2, 33; in Girl Guides, 31; school trips abroad, 31–2; 1960s teenager, 32–3, 34–6, 37–8; considers going to art school, 32; first interest in opposite sex, 32; Saturday jobs, 33–4, 37; crush on Melvyn, 37–8; quizzes brother-in-law about life in police, 36

Joins Metropolitan Police: applies to join the Metropolitan Police, 37; interviewed and examined, 40–5; vetted, 45; leaves home, 47; at Peto House, 49–53, 64, 72; at police training school (Peel House), 55–64, 65–74; relations with Graham Shepherd, 65, 75, 77, 123–5, 141; watches trials at Southwark Crown Court, 72; visits Holloway, 73; one-day placement at Walworth Police Station, 73–4; passes exams and given warrant card, 74–5; celebrations, 75

Probationer constable: posted to Romford, 76–7, 79–80; induction and familiarisation, 80–4; allocated collar number, 81, 97–8; at Upminster police hostel, 87–8, 92, 111–12, 114, 122–5, 140, 178; salary, 86–7; beat patrols, 90, 93; on night duty, 90–3; spurns advances from married colleagues, 92; initiation ceremony at mortuary, 98–9; first arrest, 99–102; continuation training 102; reprimanded for contravening hostel rules, 123–5; traffic policing duties, 130–6; holiday in Ibiza with Marilyn, 137; travels to Wales for Juvenile Court hearing, 139–40; twenty-first birthday celebrations, 140; switchboard operator duties, 140–1; relations with Charlie, 141–2; fashion-conscious, 140, 142; attends police driving course at Hendon, 151–4; buys secondhand car, 155–6; completes probation period, 157

Constable: attached to Vice Squad, 157, 158–66; heartbroken at losing Charlie, 167, 180; posted to Hornchurch, 167–9; takes radio operator training course, 173; on duty for Trooping of Colour (1971), 173–4; posted to Dagenham, 177–8; relocated to Ede Section House, 178–80; relations with Dan, 180; relations with James Easter, 193; posted to Sydenham, 183–4, 193; at Catford police hostel, 183–4, 192; acts as Juvenile Court matron, 184; driving on duty, 187; attached to prison van service (B11), 188–9; at Andy Williams concert, 191–2; gives talks to schools and other outside bodies, 193; considers career in teaching, 193; resigns from

Index

police force, 197–8; reflections on service, 199–201; marriage to James (1975), 194
Crimes and incidents dealt with: abandoned baby case (Gidea Park), 104–5; alcohol-related offences, 91–2, 93, 130, 132–3; Aliens Enquiries, 169–70; care and protection work, 84–6, 116–17, 127–9, 137–40, 144–6, 148–9, 168–9; cot death (Dagenham), 178; demonstrations and ceremonial events, 173–5; drugs raids, 109–10, 169; Eltham Well Hall train crash (1972), 189–91; missing person enquiries, 84–6, 102–3, 115–20, 127–9; prostitution and commercialised vice, 159–60, 162–6; purse-snatching, 99–102; Raphael Park 'love-in' (1967), 108–9; robbery, 94–5; Rolf Harris driving incident, 186–7; runaway horse on A127, 133–5; sexual offences, 170–1, 185–6; shoplifting offences, 171–3; strip club raid, 159–60; suicide case (Harold Hill), 148–9; surveillance at Colony Room, 161–2; theft, 187
women police: A4 Branch, 42, 62, 84, 86, 129, 197; Aliens Enquiries, 169–70; beat patrols, 93; cadets, 113; care and protection work, 93, 130, 144; careers and reasons for leaving force, 78, 112, 192; CID officers, 170.; competencies, 129; conflict management skills, 93, 147; custody of women and young persons, 97, 112; decoy operations, 170–1; domestic dispute handling, 93, 147; as drug-dog handlers, 184; entry requirements, 44–5, 49, 113; equipment and accessories, 61–2, 81, 113; feminisation, 62; height, 41, 113; history, 39–40, 47, 62, 122; initiation ceremonies, 98–9, 121; integration (1973), 197–8, 199; male officers' attitudes toward, 120, 197; married women regulations, 62; night duty and shift work, 87, 91–3, 112, 120; overtime, 96; pay and expenses, 86–7, 95–6; and pregnancy of unmarried recruits, 64; as radio transmission (RT) operators, 173; retaliatory behaviour, 121; revered, 200–1; role today, 199–200; sexual harassment and intimidation, 57, 67, 69, 98, 120–2; sexual offences, specialist role in, 68, 144, 170; as switchboard operators, 140–1; tea making duties, 120; in Traffic Division, 78, 130; typing, 121; uniforms, 43–4, 58, 61, 62, 108, 112–13; working hours, 87; 'WPC', as term, 199
women's suffrage movement, 24, 90
Wood, Lionel, 13
'WPC': as term, 199

young people: Children and Young Persons Act 1933, 68; interactions with police, 84–6, 116–17, 127–9, 137–40, 142–3, 144–6, 168–69; teenage life, 34–6; as victims of sexual assault, 144

www.ingramcontent.com/pod-product-compliance
Lightning Source LLC
Chambersburg PA
CBHW062204080426
42734CB00010B/1780